W9-BSS-028

1008 02513 3270

745.92 DAVIS
Davis, Esther
Sensational dried flowers

Central

OCT 0 8 1999

CENTRAL LIBRARY

Sensational Dried Flowers

Sensational Dried Flowers

MAKE ARRANGEMENTS SO
BEAUTIFUL THEY LOOK FRESH

ESTHER DAVIS

Rodale Press, Inc.
Emmaus, Pennsylvania

OUR PURPOSE

"We inspire and enable people to improve their lives and the world around them."

©1999 by Esther Davis
Illustrations ©1999 by Susan Egbert
Photographs ©1999 by Rodale Press, Inc.

All rights reserved. No part of this publication may be reproduced or transmitted in any form or by any means, electronic or mechanical, including photocopy, recording, or any other information storage and retrieval system, without the written permission of the publisher.

The information in this book has been carefully researched, and all efforts have been made to ensure accuracy. Rodale Press, Inc., assumes no responsibility for any injuries suffered or for damages or losses incurred during the use of or as a result of following this information. It is important to study all directions carefully before taking any action based on the information and advice presented in this book. When using any commercial product, *always* read and follow label directions. Where trade names are used, no discrimination is intended and no endorsement by Rodale Press, Inc., is implied.

Printed in the United States of America on acid-free ∞, recycled ♻ paper

Library of Congress Cataloging-in-Publication Data

Davis, Esther.
 Sensational dried flowers : arrangements so beautiful they look fresh / Esther Davis.
  p. cm.
 Includes index.
 ISBN 0-87596-800-7 (hardcover)
 1. Dried flower arrangement. I. Title.
SB449.3.D7 D28 1999
745.92—dc21   98-51246

Distributed in the book trade by St. Martin's Press

2 4 6 8 10 9 7 5 3 1 hardcover

Editors: **Marya Kissinger Amig and Mary Green**
Cover and Interior Book Designer:
  Marta Mitchell Strait
Layout Designer: **Dale Mack**
Interior Illustrator: **Susan Egbert**
Cover and Interior Photographer: **Mitch Mandel**
Photo Stylist: **Esther Davis and Patricia Field**
Photography Editor: **James A. Gallucci**
Location and Prop Assistance: **Dick Allison, Judith Damon, Bob and Helen Davis, Herb Detweiler, Cindi Lou MacMackin, Dave Ovenshire, and Carol Phillips**
Project Designer: **Esther Davis**
Copy Editors: **Erana Bumbardatore and Jennifer Hornsby**
Manufacturing Coordinator: **Patrick T. Smith**
Indexer: **Nan Badgett**
Editorial Assistance: **Susan L. Nickol**

RODALE HOME AND GARDEN BOOKS
Vice President and Editorial Director: **Margaret J. Lydic**
Managing Editor, Rodale Craft Books:
  Cheryl Winters Tetreau
Director of Design and Production: **Michael Ward**
Associate Art Director: **Patricia Field**
Production Manager: **Robert V. Anderson Jr.**
Studio Manager: **Leslie M. Keefe**
Copy Director: **Dolores Plikaitis**
Manufacturing Manager: **Mark Krahforst**
Office Manager: **Karen Earl-Braymer**

On the cover: "Sunday's Child;" see page 135

We're always happy to hear from you. For questions or comments concerning the editorial content of this book, please write to:

Rodale Press, Inc.
Book Readers' Service
33 East Minor Street
Emmaus, PA 18098

Look for other Rodale books wherever books are sold. Or call us at (800) 848-4735.

For more information about Rodale Press and the books and magazines we publish, visit our World Wide Web site at:
http://www.rodalepress.com

To my parents, Bob and Helen Davis, for the many ways they challenged me, supported me, and cheered me on.

Contents

FOUND OBJECTS   96

Almost any container you may find—from old boxes to rusty pans to odd-shaped baskets—can serve as the base for an attractive dried floral arrangement.

CONTAINER CONCEPTS   112

The color, shape, and texture of a container can play a major role in how you create your next dried floral arrangement.

TRADITION, TRADITION   130

Traditional dried floral projects don't have to be uninspiring. Use eye-catching materials and arrange them with flair.

FLOWER DRYING TIMETABLE   159

Here are my favorite time-tested tips for cleaning, sealing, and storing dried flowers.

$\mathcal{I}$ntroduction

My intrigue with flower drying began years ago when, as a child, I dried a rose from my mother's rose garden, using a 1-pound coffee can and sand from a nearby creek. I didn't come up with the idea of drying a flower like this on my own. I was inspired by an article in a *National Geographic* magazine written by a woman who lived in Salt Lake City. In her article, she explained how she used sand from the Great Salt Lake to dry flowers, and pictured was a snowman covered with zinnias—a true testament of her success.

As much as I'd like to say my career as a dried floral artist began then, it didn't. It wasn't until 10 years ago, following my move to Virginia, that I really got my hands into this business of flower drying. I started as many of you did—as a wreath maker, making wreaths from everlastings, twigs and leaves picked up from my backyard, interesting materials gathered from the wild, and whatever else I could get my hands on that looked as if it would be good wreath material. Soon I began decorating small baskets and making arrangements from these same materials, selling them from a small retail studio. Because I have always enjoyed gardening, I decided that growing my own flowers would be a good next step to take, so I dug up my then gardenless backyard and planted flowers for drying.

My gardens flourished, supplying me with an abundance of just what I needed, and it gave me a great deal of satisfaction to grow and harvest the flowers I used in my work.

After a time, however, I ran out of fresh ideas on how to creatively arrange strawflowers and German statice. I got tired of seeing every piece I made look like all the ones I had made before it. I found myself longing for a greater variety of flower shapes to work with than was afforded me with everlastings. Remembering my sand-dried rose from years ago, I began experimenting with drying flowers in several different drying mediums that were on the market at that time, and I soon found that silica gel gave me the best results. After removing a few perfectly dried flowers from this unique drying medium, I was hooked.

Although I was unable to find a lot of detailed, specific information about the use of silica gel, with persistence my flower drying successes began to outnumber my failures, and my backyard gardens of everlastings gave way to a variety of other flowers like roses, zinnias, daisies, and larkspur. Anxious to try drying anything and everything and to get the best results I possibly could, I shopped bookstores, browsed through magazines, and even searched the Internet looking for information to guide me.

To my surprise, information on this type of flower drying was limited. I would often find only a page or two out of an entire book about drying with silica gel, and often the author would refer the reader to the instructions on the back of a silica gel container for guidance. The instructions on these containers were often incomplete, though, and they often eliminated critical finishing steps that could prevent many flower drying failures.

Trial and error proved to be my best teacher, as did my desire to stick with the process until I obtained the qualities I wanted in a dried flower. I can attribute the successes I've had to having developed a very basic but critical understanding that no two flower varieties are alike. Just as I wouldn't treat them the same when growing them, or even when working with them as cut flowers in a vase, neither would I give them all the same amount of drying time in silica gel, nor would I expect them all to perform equally well as dried flowers.

You don't have to have an English garden fit for a queen to have flowers to dry. While it's nice to have days when the garden will give you a dozen perfect roses or 10 stalks of delphinium that are ready to be picked all at once, the flowers from my garden are often gleaned one at a time, and I have to be willing to work with them as they are offered.

You'll need to develop a gentle touch when working with flowers dried in silica gel. While air-dried flowers are sturdy little things, these flowers often are not, and careful handling will pay off.

If you've never dried a flower in your life, or if your success with drying flowers has been limited, this book is for you. If you enjoy gardening and arranging flowers, this book will provide you with a new way to display your flowers all year long. Even though the projects range from very simple pieces to those that are more involved, the flowers that I used in them were all dried by the same technique. Once you have mastered that technique, the sky's the limit. My arrangements are here for you to copy or to give you ideas on how to incorporate the flowers and materials you have available to you into unique designs of your own. I didn't master this craft overnight and you probably won't either, but I encourage you to stay with it. The results will be truly rewarding!

Esther Davis

The Art of Drying

"THEY LOOK SO REAL!" I hear this comment whenever people discover that the flowers in my arrangements are dried. But the flowers *are* real, and what people really mean is that they look so *fresh*. Often, dried floral arrangements are composed of everlasting flowers, so when people see my arrangements, their reaction is one of disbelief ("These can't be dried!"), amazement ("These *are* dried!"), and wonder ("How did you do this?"). But you don't have to limit yourself to working with everlastings (the flowers typically used for drying, like statice and strawflowers). A wide variety of the flowers and greenery that surround you are suitable for drying.

I achieve the realistic look of fresh flowers by drying my blooms and foliage in silica gel. Although the technology of using a desiccant, such as silica gel, as a flower-drying agent has been available for some time, it is a process that is often admired but seldom tried. You may have a book on flower drying that has a page or two of instructions on using desiccants, so you may have been enticed to go out and buy a container of silica gel. Like many others, you may have tried to dry a few flowers but were unsuccessful, and since then, the container of desiccant has been relegated to a shelf in your pantry. If this has happened to you, take heart. Many other floral designers have done the same.

Although drying with silica gel isn't difficult, it requires patience and a willingness to try and try again. All flowers are different sizes, shapes, and densities, and all of these factors influence the drying time for each bloom. What I do for you in this book is take the guesswork out of what those drying times are and solve some of the other mysteries surrounding drying flowers with a desiccant.

When you begin to dry flowers, particularly in silica gel, allow yourself time to become acquainted with the process. Don't plan on making a project for a special occasion until you've honed your skills. My skill at drying flowers is an acquired one, and with each attempt my skills improve.

If you want to become skilled at drying flowers, you will find that you have to become a servant to these fragile beauties. You must grow flowers so their petals are unblemished and handle them with an unhurried, gentle hand during the drying process. You must store the flowers so they are kept dry and give each petal adequate preparation before working them into a finished piece. Then, you must care for the flowers while they are displayed, making sure their environment suits their needs. If you do these things, your dried flowers will fill your home with the same joy and beauty that fresh-cut flowers provide.

After you have spent hours drying flowers, treat them gently and store them where they will be kept dry.

Start with What You Have

BEFORE YOU RUSH OUT to buy a variety of flowering plants to dry, go out into your garden and take inventory of what you have. You may find that materials you never would have considered drying are actually very good candidates. Do you have flowering spring bulbs that put on a showy display? Do you have any blooming shrubs with blossoms that could be snipped off and dried by themselves or on the branch? Do you have trees or bushes that have interesting foliage? What about groundcovers that might make attractive fillers? And don't overlook the materials that are often a nuisance when they fall and fill up the yard, like the centers of spent magnolia blossoms, leaves, and pinecones.

If you plant flowers in your garden specifically for drying, remember that some flowers will come out of the drying medium slightly darker than

Many of the annuals and perennials growing right in my own yard are great flowers for drying.

when they went in (see "Flower Drying Timetable" on page 159), so you may want to purchase flowers a shade or two lighter than you'd like them to be when dried. A nice medium pink zinnia will become hot pink when dried, while lavenders may become purple, and a deep red rose will turn a dark burgundy. To find the varieties that you like, you may have to check out a number of seed catalogs, or ask your local nursery or mail-order plant supplier to make a special order for you. This will be worth the effort.

When selecting your garden flowers and plants for drying, you'll want to give them extra care. The goal is to have as perfect a blossom as you can grow because any blemishes on the flower petals are going to be made more obvious by the drying process. Be sure to keep your garden free of insects and disease, and stop overhead watering. After a good rain, I even go out and shake the water off the hydrangea heads, particularly if they are in a sunny spot. The combination of raindrops and sunshine may discolor flower heads because the water lying on the petals acts as a magnifying glass, intensifying the sun's rays, which burns the petals.

CUTTING FLOWERS FOR DRYING

If you grow fresh flowers that you cut and bring indoors, chances are you already have what you need to cut the flowers for drying. The tools I use most often are a one-gallon pail with a handle, small glass bottles or aluminum cans of various sizes, garden clippers, and my thumb and index finger.

I sometimes gather flowers for drying in a basket like this. When I get the flowers inside, I recut the stems about 1 inch up from the end and place them in water. Sometimes I carry a cutting bucket with water to the garden so I can place the stems in water immediately.

It is best to cut a fresh flower when it is turgid, or as full of moisture as possible in its stem, petals, and leaves. That is what you want to capture when you select a flower to dry. As a summer day warms up, a plant begins to transpire, or lose moisture from its surfaces into the surrounding air, thereby gradually losing its turgidity through the day. As the temperature cools down in the evening, the transpiration rate slows, and the plant builds up its moisture content overnight and repeats this cycle the next day. This means that flowers are in their peak form first thing in the morning, which would be the ideal time to cut them if it weren't for the presence of dew on the petals, leaves, and stems. So, I usually wait until midmorning to do my cutting because I find that the flowers are usually nice and crisp, and a lot of the dew has evaporated. I also cut later in the evening.

If a flower is slightly wilted when you put it into the silica gel, it will be harder to get the particles between the petals, which will make it harder to preserve the nice, fresh shape you'll want the flower to have in its dried form.

I have noticed that some flowers lose moisture less rapidly during the day, and with these I'll risk cutting the flowers almost any time of day. For example, zinnias and rudbeckias seem to be perky most any time, and if they're going to go right into the silica gel, I usually cut them whenever it suits me. To be able to cut your flowers in their peak form, you must become acquainted with the changes in petal texture by feeling them at different times during the day. Also, experiment by cutting them for drying at different times. Temperature and humidity conditions vary all across the country, and what doesn't work in my garden may very well work in yours.

I tend my gardens with loving care, and in return they provide me with a bounty of flowers to dry.

Short-Stemmed Flowers

When I cut short-stemmed or delicately stemmed flowers, such as pansies, I snip them off above the foliage, and I place them in a flat basket. I take the basket indoors, recut the stems, and place them in containers of water. I have accumulated quite a collection of small glass bottles that hold the little blossoms. I insert larger, flat-headed flowers, like zinnias, into a grid made out of chicken wire that I place over a flat cake pan or shallow plastic container filled with water. This holds them nicely until they are ready to be covered with silica gel.

Sometimes I walk through my garden with no intention of cutting any flowers. But I often spot a zinnia that is too perfect to leave, so I snip it off with my thumb and index finger. (I've developed a new appreciation for the term "green thumb.") However, during the evening hours, bumblebees lurk in my zinnias, often attaching themselves to the underside of petals, settling in for the night. Because I'm not using clippers and the light is fading, my unsuspecting fingers find the bumble-bees. So if you are overcome by unplanned clipping urges in the evening hours, be careful!

Long-Stemmed Flowers

When I go out into my garden to gather long-stemmed flowers, I place several smaller containers or vases of water inside the one-gallon pail. As I cut the flowers, I strip off the lower leaves and then place the stems in the small containers. This way, the flowers stay upright and don't get squashed. Plus, the lower blossoms on spiky flowers like lark-spur stay dry and are easier to remove from the pail without damaging the blossoms.

Sometimes, however, I just lay roses and other long-stemmed flowers in a flat basket as I cut them. Inside the house, I strip off the lower leaves, remove rose thorns, recut the stems, and place them in water.

While there will always be "ideal" ways to work with fresh flowers, you need to know that deviating from these methods, whether they are mine or someone else's, will not necessarily result in disaster. Flowers are often more resilient than we think.

GATHERING FOLIAGE FOR DRYING

Seldom do I put together a dried floral piece without somehow incorporating foliage of some kind, be it only a few sprigs of boxwood tucked in here and there on a wreath or longer, more graceful branches of flowering quince to help define the shape of a larger, more elegant arrangement. Not only does foliage give life to flowers in the garden, it is also an element that gives life to a dried floral piece, often transforming a dull, muted piece into one that looks as if it had just been picked from the garden.

When choosing foliage to integrate into floral pieces, I look for plants that have nice, firm or leathery-feeling leaves, such as forsythia, peony, or boxwood. Foliage of this type won't be as fragile to the touch after it has been dried in silica gel, and it will be less likely to droop if exposed to moisture. Because mature leaves have a more leathery feel to them than young leaves, I also like to wait until foliage ages a bit before cutting it to dry. Unfortunately, a lot of flower foliage doesn't meet the ideal criteria for drying, but because of its coloring, shape, or the fact that it belongs with a particular chosen flower, I dry it anyway. This foliage may not hold up as well as other types, but it will look nice for a while and can always be replaced later if it droops or fades.

Leaves or foliage with a high moisture content—those we might consider spongy in texture, like a begonia leaf, rather than crisp, like ivy—will respond to silica gel drying in the same way as flowers with high moisture content. Their beautiful green coloring will give way to a tan or brown coloring, and the leaves may become so papery thin that they are virtually unusable. Leaves on the stem of a lily, tulip, or daffodil will lose their color, but when they're dry, they will retain a rigid enough form for you to spray color back onto the leaves if you want to use them with their flower.

I take a lot of liberties with the use of foliage and often substitute foliage that looks like the leaves of a particular flower instead of that flower's

Don't overlook grasses, foliage, and other materials for your drying projects. They can be used to fill out an arrangement or wreath nicely and can add an interesting touch of color.

actual leaves. Single peony leaves or those from a forsythia branch can be added back to a lily stem, and at a glance, one probably wouldn't realize they were a substitute for the real thing. Adding nice, crisp pachysandra leaves to the base of a grouping of pansies or primroses is a good replacement for the more fragile leaves of those flowers.

Don't forget to cut foliage in the fall, too. The color changes occurring in leaves can be captured with silica gel drying, and the leaves will be beautiful additions to floral pieces. If you can snip off leaf branches in the early stages of the color changes, the leaves will be less likely to come loose from the branch after it is dry.

*L*ook Beyond Your Garden

WHEN YOU LOOK FOR FLOWERS and foliage to dry, remember that a lot of excellent materials can be found outside of your own garden. I've met many nice people with lots of pretty flowers in their yards by knocking on doors and asking if I might have a blossom or two of something that caught my eye. When I explain what I do, people are usually very generous with the bounty of their gardens. Plus, they often give me a blossom or leaf that I've never dried before.

I have favorite fields and roadside areas where I routinely gather flowers and foliage. Goldenrod, Queen-Anne's-lace, grasses, and rose hips are some lovely materials that are available in the wild. Of course, I never gather endangered or protected plant species, and I don't trespass on private property.

Supplement flowers you have in your garden by asking neighbors and friends for samples, and keep an eye out for interesting materials when you're walking or hiking.

When I visit my parents in Washington State during the summer, I make a point to gather native materials from the pasture and hillside behind their house. Variety is the spice of life, and it can often be the spice of a dried floral arrangement as well. Since many of the materials I gather in Washington are often already dried by the hot summer sun, I carefully box them and ship them home. you're far from home and something you've gathered isn't dry, be sure to dry it before it

YOU CAN SHIP THAT HYDRANGEA, BUT DRY IT FIRST!

Several years ago I visited out-of-state relatives who generously cut the heads off their beautiful blue hydrangea bush for me to take back to Virginia for drying. I was driving, so I placed the flower heads in a black plastic garbage bag that I put on top of my luggage in the back seat of the car. I had to make a stop on the way home, so the hydrangeas were closed up in their plastic bag in the car for several hours. It was a very hot day. As you can imagine, the car got quite warm inside, the moist hydrangeas in their black plastic bag got even warmer, and by the time I arrived home, the once-beautiful blue hydrangea heads were now rather tan and cooked looking—not a pretty sight. Had I spread out the hydrangeas all over the interior of the car and cracked the windows so the moisture had some way to escape, the results might have been much different. Remember, warm, dry environments work well for flower drying; hot, moist ones do not.

is shipped, or you will most likely be disappointed with the condition of the material when it arrives at your home.

Don't forget to check your local florists, greenhouses, and grocery stores for interesting flowers and distinctive foliage. Of course, growing your own flowers is less expensive than buying them—and for those of you who are fond of gardening, more fun—but sometimes you may need a special color or flower you don't have, and florists, greenhouses, and grocery stores may have just what you need.

CHOOSE PREDRIED MATERIALS WITH CARE

Many prepackaged, dried materials that were once only available seasonally at craft stores are now available year-round. You can often find a nice variety of everlasting flowers, preserved greenery, and other materials in the craft store chains. Occasionally, I even see packaged flower heads that have been freeze-dried.

In the summertime, several individuals who grow everlastings sell their harvests at our local farmers' market, as may happen in your area. As I pass their displays, I have a hard time resisting the brightly colored bunches of strawflowers or globe amaranth. A mix of prepackaged everlastings and other materials can combine nicely with your garden flowers if you're careful when you select the prepackaged material. If you make your purchases from a craft store, avoid material that has been placed near large glass windows where direct sunlight could hit it. Strong sunlight adds months of age to the material, fading the green stems and leaves and washing out the color of the flower heads even before you take it off the shelf. If you see any tiny moths flitting around the material, be aware that the material may contain eggs laid by those moths, and your dried material may be a meal for the larvae when they hatch. If there are some small shattered pieces of dried material at the bottom of the plastic sleeve surrounding the material, it may be the result of rough handling, or a moth might have been at work already.

Not all, but a lot, of the dried material that is sold in craft stores is grown overseas and imported. Before you take it off the shelf, it might have changed hands three to five times between the grower and the retailer. Dried materials are usually purchased by retail stores in cases that are tightly packed and sealed, so often the most and the worst handling the material will receive will be at the craft store as the material is unpacked and shelved by hasty hands. Always choose quality material. It will pay off for you.

Setting Up a Workspace

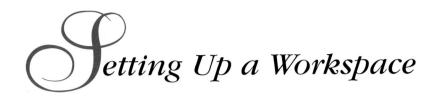

ONE OF THE BIGGEST SURPRISES I had when I began drying flowers was how much room was taken up by all of the processes involved. I'd start with a pail of cut flowers in water, and pretty soon countertops were covered with boxes of drying flowers, containers of silica gel, and containers of dried flowers. When I ran out of counter space, I started piling up boxes on the floor. I hung foliage or flowers that I was air drying from clotheslines I'd strung across my ceiling. When the clotheslines were filled, I hung materials from the tops of cupboard doors, the backs of chairs, and the edges of countertops.

This scenario probably won't be yours. Dried flowers are, after all, my business. But be aware that this craft will demand some space, so think about what corner of your home or garage you can dedicate to it. If you have family members to

Be sure to set aside plenty of space for your flower-drying activities. A long countertop or table that's at a comfortable height for you when standing will guard against back strain.

11

consider, especially small children, or if you have indoor pets, select a spot that will be safe from wagging tails or little bodies running around. An unintentional brush of your hand can accidentally knock a petal loose from a dried flower. Think what could happen if your kitty should jump up on the counter when you're not looking in order to taste or play with the arrangement you just finished! If you place flowers in containers of silica gel for drying, they need to be put in a spot where they will be undisturbed. A drastic shift of silica gel around a flower will cause the contour of the flower to change.

You must also make sure your workspace is well ventilated. Pouring silica gel around flowers to be dried and off of flowers that are dry will generate a fine dust. When pouring it from a container onto a cookie sheet for redrying, for example, you may not be able to see any visible dust, but it is there. If you work with silica gel frequently, you

will soon be able to detect a fine film of dust covering everything in the room. One of my solutions was a rather cramped one, but it worked.

Before I moved my workspace to my farmhouse, I worked in a two-story brick house. At the top of the stairway leading from the kitchen to the basement I had a door I could close. Halfway down the stairway there was a 3-foot-square landing with a door leading outside. I had a carpenter attach a 1½ × 2-foot piece of plywood to the wall of the landing with hinges, so the plywood could drop down for a work surface and fold up and out of the way against the wall when not in use. That gave me a surface just large enough to do my silica gel work. There was standing room for me right in front of the exterior door, which I opened to let out the dust.

I also strongly recommend that when working with silica gel, you wear a mask that covers your nose and mouth so that you don't breathe in the

As you can see, my kitchen is my drying workshop. Having the sink and oven nearby means I can work more efficiently when filling pails with water and redrying silica gel.

dust. When purchasing a mask, read the package to make sure the mask you choose filters out silica gel dust. Some do not. Mine is a hefty mask that has filters I can change.

CONSIDER YOUR KITCHEN

My favorite spot to work is still in my kitchen. Virtually every appliance in my kitchen is of use to me, with the exception of the microwave and dishwasher.

The sink is a water source from which I fill my cutting pails and my teakettle. I use the stove to heat the water in the teakettle to create steam; this and my glue gun are the key tools for doing design work. I use the oven to redry silica gel, and I often use the refrigerator to house some cut flowers overnight. I also place air-dried material in the freezer to kill any pests that may be hiding down between the petals.

If you decide to work in your kitchen, you may be tempted to use the exhaust fan above your stove to clear the air of silica dust. Unfortunately, that means working on top of the burners. The fan filters, which may already have cooking grease on them, are going to attract the dust instead of allowing the fan to exhaust it out of the house. If you choose to work under your kitchen stove fan, make sure that the fan carries exhaust to the outside of your home and doesn't just circulate it back into the interior of your kitchen. Also, make sure you keep the filters clean.

GOOD LIGHTING IS A MUST

One reason I choose to work in my kitchen and dining area is because of the wonderful daylight that streams in through the windows. Good lighting is essential. There is no artificial light that compares to the light of day. If you are working on small items, lighting isn't as critical, but for a large arrangement or wreath, good lighting will help you judge depth, balance, and density more accurately, as well as enable you to read color more accurately. I do all of my design work during the day, when I have the best light. It makes a difference not only in how the finished piece looks but also in how quickly I am able to put it together.

If possible, position your work station so that, in addition to overhead lighting, natural light comes in from behind you, as opposed to in front of you or from one side. If you work into the light, it may be very difficult to see the piece you're working on clearly, even if you have overhead lighting. If light comes in from one side, your work will be much more visible on the side that is well-lit than on the one that is not. If you move the piece to another place with different lighting conditions, inevitably, the poorly lit side will have elements about it that you'll want to change. Before you deem a piece "finished," place it in several different locations around your house, each with a different lighting condition, and take a careful look at it. You'll be amazed at the things you'll want to correct or change that were not apparent to you while you were working.

If possible, work against a blank wall. It will allow you to see the true shape of the piece or arrangement and will eliminate anything that you would see and visually read into the actual shape of the piece. If you don't have a blank wall available, create one by removing a wall decoration. Or prop up a piece of cardboard against a countertop appliance to create a blank vertical surface to work against. Even when I make a wreath, I do it against a vertical surface so I can stand back and look at my work. I sometimes find that what I thought up close were carefully placed flowers will read as loud blobs of color from a distance, creating visual imbalance.

Tools of the Trade

TO CREATE GORGEOUS dried-flower arrangements, you only need a few basic tools. Gather all of these together before you begin to work.

To keep spray paint off your hands, use a **clothespin** to grasp a short-stemmed flower, or wear **latex gloves.** If you don't own latex gloves, slip a long, thin plastic bag over your arm and hand.

Use 20- and 26-gauge **paddle wire** to make hangers for wreaths and other wall pieces. Use **green 30-gauge wrapped beading wire** to tie one piece of material tightly to another.

Use a **funnel, spoon, or measuring cup** with a handle to pour silica gel over flowers in a low, flat container.

A **floral pick** is an ideal tool for inserting stems into floral foam. The wire on the pick is wound around the base of a stem, and the pick is then inserted into the foam.

If you want to perk up the color of a dried flower or change the color entirely, use specially formulated **floral spray paints.** These paints are available in craft stores and come in a wide variety of colors. To help keep moisture and humidity off the petals of your arrangement, spray it with a low-gloss **clear acrylic spray.**

Use **wire cutters** to cut hangers for your wall arrangements and to cut ends of stem materials. Use **needle-nose pliers** to tighten the wire holding wreath bases together or to assist in making wire hangers.

Use **floral tape** to tape flower stems, and use **transparent tape** for ribbon work and bunching small stems together.

Silica gel is the medium used for drying flowers.

If you want to add extra weight to a container so it won't tip over, place **rocks** between the floral foam and the inside edge of the container. To cover the foam and rocks, use **Spanish moss** that has been dyed green.

Save space by using **clear plastic stackable containers** for drying as well as storing flowers.

KRYLON
Crystal Clear Acrylic Coating

DESIGN MASTER®
Cranberry
713

When silica gel needs redrying, spread it on a **jelly-roll pan** (a cookie sheet with sides that are about 1 inch high). When you remove dried flowers from silica gel, pour the silica gel onto these sheets.

Fabric scissors are used to cut ribbon, while small, sharply pointed scissors are used to remove the stamens of flowers and to trim petals. Use **serrated kitchen shears** for trimming leaves.

Use **play sand** to clean newly dried flowers. It gently knocks silica gel residue from the petals.

Small **watercolor or cosmetic brushes** are perfect for absorbing water from the petals of freshly picked flowers and for cleaning silica gel dust off flower petals after they're dry.

The steam generated by boiling water inside a **teakettle** is used to bend stems, fluff up flower heads, and loosen desiccant particles from the heads of dried flowers.

Floral foam holds dried flowers in their containers while you make arrangements. Select either the type that is very soft and is used for fresh flower arrangements or a slightly firmer version designed for silk and dried flowers. It's also handy to use floral foam to hold dried flowers with short stems upright while you are creating your pieces.

You will use a hot- or low-temperature **glue gun** in a variety of ways when creating dried flower arrangements. Hot glue will set up faster than a low-temperature glue and is easy to clean up.

DUAL-TEMPER G760S
CAUTION: 120V 40W E101363

ALLOW ROOM
FOR AIR DRYING

Although I use silica gel for drying most of my live materials, there are some materials that I simply air-dry. Everlastings, grasses, some types of greenery, and hydrangeas are a few examples. Materials that are air-dried must be hung upside down while drying so the stems will dry straight and the flower heads won't flop over. An ideal place to air-dry material is in an attic. Attics often lack a lot of light and are usually quite warm, especially in the summertime, when flowers are ready to harvest. The warmer the temperature, obviously, the faster the material will dry. The absence of light has nothing to do with the drying, but the lower the light level, the less the material will fade. Hence, any drying instructions will tell you to hang materials in a warm, dry, and dark place.

When I air-dry floral materials, I hang them upside down so the stems and flower heads dry straight.

However, the attic is a less-than-ideal spot for drying if you live in a climate that is particularly humid. The humidity outside of a home is generally present on the inside of a home to a somewhat lesser degree, unless it is removed by means of a dehumidifier or air conditioner. If you want plant material to dry, the moisture needs to go somewhere, and if the air is already saturated with moisture, as it would be on a rainy or highly humid day, there is nowhere for the plant moisture to go, and the material will mildew. If you live in the South, mid-Atlantic states, on a seacoast, or anywhere else that is humid, I strongly suggest that you monitor the humidity. I have a humidity gauge—in fact, several of them. They are inexpensive and can be purchased in a hardware or variety store. I like to keep the humidity level at 60 percent or lower. Flowers will stay dry at that level, and it's one at which most of us are comfortable.

If an attic isn't available to you, other places will do just fine for drying, provided they are dry, relatively warm places. In my first house, I used my 9-foot kitchen ceiling. I strung heavy cording from one wall to the other and hung bunches of flowers and other plant materials from the cording. Often the weight of the materials hanging from the cording would weigh it down so much that I'd find myself bumping into them, but I reached the point where I instinctively knew where to dodge or duck. Another drawback was, of course, that the materials were not in a dark place, and every time I turned on the kitchen light, they were exposed to it. But believe it or not, that didn't end my flower-drying career. In fact, I found that when I left dried material up where it could easily be seen and accessed, I used it more often. As much as I'd recommend taking down dried materials and storing them in a box, my way did have distinct advantages.

If you don't have 9-foot ceilings or an attic, improvise. Stretch drying lines around the perimeter of a room (where they will be out of the way) instead of through the center of it. How about using a clothes rack? Or empty a closet, and hang bunches from clothes hangers.

WATCH OUT FOR INSECTS

Whether you purchase dried materials, grow or gather your own, or work with them strictly for your own pleasure or as a business, you will undoubtedly have to deal with pests of some kind at some point. I know of one reputable dried-flower distributor who fumigated regularly with a substance strong enough to kill rats, yet they discontinued carrying dried fruit slices because he couldn't keep them pest-free. I know another woman who, during a European visit, purchased hundreds of dollars' worth of dried floral pieces that had to be thrown away when she got them home because they were all literally being eaten. Although these are two very different scenarios, they illustrate that dried flower pests can affect anyone anywhere.

It isn't my intent to make you so concerned about insects as you work with dried flowers that you stop working with natural materials. But I want to give you some real straight talk about pests. If you are aware that you need to watch for them and are given appropriate ways to control them, pests need not be a worry at all.

Because commercial growers and distributors fumigate for pests on a regular basis using sophisticated commercial techniques, it's safe to say that most material you purchase will probably be pest-free. However, some pests will occasionally be alive and well or ready to hatch in the material you purchase. In all fairness to the grower, distributor, and retailer, it's hard to know where in the chain of distribution the infestation occurred.

Material harvested from your garden or gathered from the wild isn't always pest-free, either. While drying flowers in silica gel will smother any insects or larvae that may be hidden down inside the petals, if you air-dry flowers, any pests that are tucked down inside the flower, feasting on it, will continue to feast as the flower is drying and after it has dried. When the pests have consumed all that tastes good to them, they will move on to another flower, if available. In the process, they may find mates and create more bugs, and pretty soon there will be a full-scale banquet going on. The first clue that you have a pest problem is when you see fallen petals on your countertops accompanied by tiny insect droppings.

Air-dried peonies and roses seem to be particularly attractive to insects. However, adult pests, their eggs, and larvae can usually be eradicated by exposure to temperatures that are extremely hot or cold for them. This means that if you place air-dried materials in a freezer for about a week and then in a 140°F oven for an hour, chances are good that you will kill any living pests present in the materials. It doesn't mean, however, that these materials won't still be susceptible to infestation from pests from other materials, so when storing them, you must make sure you place them in containers that will keep them protected.

Be diligent about checking any stored air-dried materials frequently, and if you find something being eaten, it's best to get rid of it. Ideally, you should store air-dried or glycerin-preserved (as in the case of preserved greenery) materials in closed boxes, and if you see even an occasional moth flitting around, go through your boxes immediately to see if you can locate the source. There usually will be one somewhere, easily identifiable by moths or larvae and shattered material. If your moth problem seems to be isolated to one box, a good precautionary measure is to seal all the other boxes with tape. It will be less handy for you to retrieve dried materials from a box sealed with tape, but it will also make it harder for insects to get to your materials. If you suspect that you may have an insect problem, putting up with a few precautionary inconveniences early on may save you a lot of destroyed material later. For example, if you have taken dried materials out of containers to work them into floral pieces, don't leave the leftovers out. Keep the materials protected by returning them to their boxes or containers as soon as your piece is finished.

Moths

The meal moth and the Mediterranean flour moth are particularly bothersome pests. The larvae of these moths feed on grains, cereals, wool, and dried flowers. Adult moths are tiny and prefer dark, tight places. They lay eggs anywhere they think there will be a food source for the tiny larvae when they hatch. The larvae hatch from the eggs, eat, spin cocoons, hatch into moths, and the cycle is repeated. Tightly bunched and packaged materials, such as you may purchase, are a great source of food for them. Where flower stems are tied together is a dense, dark area that may go undisturbed for a long period of time. These are ideal conditions for larvae to live and

Seven Ways to Control *Pests*

1 Keep your garden as insect-free as you possibly can. Check over blossoms before you bring them into the house. Remove any insects or spiders you see. Look over any materials gathered from the wild, as well.

2 Assume all material you bring in to air-dry may have pests present. Freeze and/or heat air-dried flowers or gathered materials after they are dry to kill any pests that may be present.

3 Look for signs of pests in any materials you consider purchasing from a store before you buy them.

4 Keep dried materials in containers with lids or in boxes you can close up tightly.

5 Check stored dried materials frequently. Discard anything that's being eaten by insects or larvae.

6 Return any leftover dried materials to their boxes after you have finished working with them. Don't leave them out, even if it's just overnight.

7 Purchase sticky moth traps and place them near items that may be susceptible to infestation.

feed in. Another thing to be aware of is that although larvae will leave some flowers alone, like annual statice, they will feast on the pulp up inside the stem, entering from the bottom. Although this doesn't ruin the flower head, it does allow the life cycle of the moth to continue. If you were to place a piece of affected statice in a dried wreath, for example, the moth larvae could conceivably move on to anything else in the wreath that was edible, and that would be the end of the wreath.

If material in a wreath is suspiciously shattering, here is a test you can do to determine if it is an insect problem. Hold the wreath face down by its base over a clean countertop without letting it rest on the counter. (You may need an extra hand, so it's best to have someone help you with this.) Lightly slap the back of the base with your hand all the way around the wreath. Then look to see what you have knocked loose. If larvae or insects are present, they will be knocked onto the counter, as will any of their droppings. If no larvae, insects, or droppings appear, it's safe to assume the wreath material is just overly dry.

If you have a moth problem, be aware that even materials stored in plastic bags will be susceptible to their invasion. Moths can also eat through aluminum foil. Only airtight containers with tight-fitting lids will keep moths out.

One way to fight moth infestation is by using traps that have a sticky inside surface and a pheromone packet that attracts adult moths. The moths fly into the trap, get stuck, and die before they can lay eggs. These traps can often be found in organic gardening catalogs and at garden centers.

While the labels on mothballs and cedar blocks or shavings may claim that they will kill adult moths, my experience is that they won't do this unless the environment they're placed in is airtight. Mothballs will only drive a moth to another source, and mothballs can be toxic to children and pets.

Beetles

A less common pest problem, but one that bears mentioning, is that of wood-eating beetles. A friend of mine sent me an article that appeared in her local newspaper about a lady who unknowingly had the unfortunate experience of purchasing several premade grapevine wreath bases infected with powder post beetles. She decorated the bases, giving some away as gifts to friends and keeping one for herself. After her wreath had decorated her dining room table for a party and had then been hanging for display in her home for a while, she began to notice that the wreath materials began to look prematurely dusty and that there was a pile of sawdust on the floor under the wreath. She got rid of the wreath. Her friends had also commented to her that the wreaths she had so lovingly made for them had needed to be tossed as well. As if this in itself wasn't enough, the beetles had migrated to the legs of her hardwood dining room table and set up camp there! It wasn't a pretty sight.

The very week I received that article, I had purchased some grapevine wreaths from a supplier, and as I retrieved one, I noticed a small amount of sawdust on top of the surface it had been lying on. "Ah ha," I thought. Indeed, on closer inspection of the wreath, I noticed holes the size of the push-button end of a ballpoint pen in the wreath. How timely for me to have just received that article! During all of the time I had been working with dried flowers, that was the first and only time, to my knowledge, that I had ever purchased infested wreath bases, and fortunately, I was lucky.

For more information on organic moth and pest controls, contact your County Cooperative Extension Service. It often has helpful information about household pest control. Again, don't be intimidated by pests. Just be on the lookout for them, and know there are steps you can take to eliminate them.

Using Silica Gel

EACH OF US, AT ONE TIME or another, has encountered a mysterious little package of crystals in the box of a new pair of shoes, a kitchen appliance, or a radio. That little package was filled with silica gel, put there to do what it does best—absorb any moisture that may work its way into the box between the time the item is packaged and the time it is purchased. Silica gel is known as a desiccant, or a drying agent, and while the silica gel used to dry flowers is ground much more finely than what is inside those little packages, it is the same product and is used for the same purpose—to absorb moisture.

Silica gel was used in science and industry as a desiccant long before anyone discovered that it could be used successfully to dry flowers. Many other agents that were used to dry flowers, such as borax and cornmeal, gave way to silica gel in the 1950s and '60s as companies began to manufacture it specifically for flower-drying purposes.

Instead of being solid, a little particle of silica gel is actually very porous. If you looked at it under a microscope, you would see a lot of little pockets on its surface. If you sliced it open, you'd see that those little pockets on the surface actually go all the way through the particle and are interconnected. This means that silica gel has a large surface area. Each of those little pockets attracts and holds moisture, and the pockets enable the particle of silica gel to hold 40 to 50 percent of its own weight in moisture. Plus, it will hold that moisture until it is heated to a temperature at which the moisture evaporates. Silica gel doesn't even necessarily have to be surrounding something to dry it out. If you were to take the lid off a container of dry silica gel and leave it sitting on your kitchen counter, it would absorb any moisture that was present in the air.

When silica gel has absorbed moisture, it doesn't feel moist to the touch. So how do you determine when the material you're drying is

WHY A PARTICLE IS CALLED A GEL

Because silica gel resembles table sugar, its name often causes quite a bit of confusion. Unlike the mineral silica that is mined and used in glass making, this silica is what is known as a chemical compound, which is made from mixing chemicals and other ingredients together. In the case of silica gel, two chemical solutions—sodium silicate and sulfuric acid—are mixed together with water to form a gel, or very thick solution. The acid is removed and the gel is baked, causing the water to evaporate. Tiny particles, or a precipitate, is left behind. This is called silica gel. The particles are then ground to different sizes that vary from coarse to fine. It is the fine particles that are used to dry flowers.

really dry? Particles of cobalt chloride are added to the silica gel that is sold for flower drying. When the silica gel is dry, these particles are blue. When the silica gel is full of moisture, they turn pink. You'll know when the silica gel is full of moisture when you no longer see any blue particles. Before using the silica gel again, you must dry it in the oven until the blue particles reappear. If you purchase a container of silica gel and fail to see any blue particles, stir it up; they may be down inside the container. If, after stirring, you still fail to see any blue, the silica gel will need to be dried before you use it.

Carefully sift silica gel over flowers when covering them for drying so they retain their form and aren't matted down by the weight of too much silica gel being poured at once.

$\mathcal{S}$tarting the Drying Process

YOU'LL BE SUCCESSFUL when drying with silica gel if you choose your flowers carefully (see "Cutting Flowers for Drying" on page 4), dry them for the correct amount of time, clean them thoroughly, and properly care for them once they are dried.

The time it takes a flower to dry is determined by several things—how large it is, how densely packed the petals are, how large and thick the petals are, what the consistency of the calyx is, how dense its center is, and what time of day it is picked. Although many varieties of flowers are similar in many of these characteristics, no two are exactly alike, so each flower has to be evaluated on an individual basis when determining a drying time. A pansy or a cosmos can take three days to dry, while a nice dense rose can take two weeks.

DRYING A SINGLE BLOSSOM

The blossoms you choose to dry should be in perfect condition. Often a dried flower in its most perfect form isn't going to look quite as perky as it did when it was fresh, and any blemish is going to be more obvious once the flower is dried. The

I try to select flowers for drying that are as blemish-free as possible. Any flaw in the petals will only be more obvious after the flower has dried.

easiest way to achieve perfect blossoms is to control pests and diseases and to pick flowers before they endure a rainstorm. If flowers, such as roses, are too mature and open, they may lose their petals while being removed from the silica gel. Some years, it can be a struggle to find perfect blossoms, and if you are having a bad garden year, you'll just have to do the best you can. I've had thrip on my Shasta daisies, too many Japanese beetles eating my roses, and powdery mildew on my zinnias all at once, and that year I learned to improvise a lot! Drying a less-than-perfect blossom doesn't mean the result will be a total failure. The flower may not be nearly as pretty as it might have been under more ideal conditions, though.

When I have a cut flower sitting in water on my kitchen counter, the first thing I do to prepare it for drying is to make sure the petals are completely dry and dew-free. Any moisture left on a petal is apt to discolor the petal during the drying process, so if the petals are not dry, I remove lingering dewdrops with a small, soft watercolor or cosmetic brush. After each dewdrop is removed, I squeeze the moisture from the brush using a folded paper towel or tissue. On multipetaled flowers such as roses, especially ones that haven't opened all the way, I'm careful to search between the petals and into the tighter center for dewdrops as best I can, because they love to hide there.

Next, I cut the flower from its stem, leaving its receptacle (if it has one) and sepals intact, as shown in **Diagram 1.** I also leave a tiny bit of stem to help the flower stay upright when I stand it in the silica gel in the bottom of the container.

If I want to insert a wire into the stem, I do that now (see "Adding a Stem" on page 38). To prepare the wire, I cut a 1½- to 2-inch piece of floral wire and bend one end over ½ inch, as shown in **Diagram 2.** Then I insert the straight end of the

wire into the center of the flower, pulling the wire through the flower and the stem until the top of the bent end is embedded in the flower head.

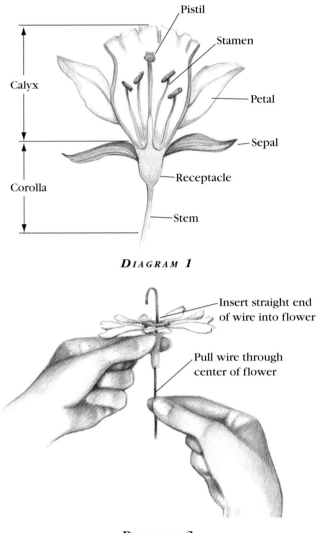

DIAGRAM 1

DIAGRAM 2

When selecting a container for drying, I try to choose containers that are close in size to the diameter of the flower so that I don't have to use any more silica gel than necessary. I then pour silica gel into the bottom of the container until it is as deep as the stem and receptacle, and I carefully place the flower in the silica gel, burying the stem and receptacle. By doing this, the flower will remain upright while I cover it.

When drying flowers like zinnias, which have many petals, I pour in the first layer of silica gel, and then I pour a small mound of silica gel on top of the first layer. Next, I insert the zinnia. The mound helps support the bottom of the flower, which will be difficult to get to as I add the rest of the silica gel, and it will prevent the flower from drying flat.

I then begin to gently spoon or pour silica gel around and between the petals of the flower so that the flower retains its original form as I pour. On flat-headed flowers that are daisy-shape, I use the end of a small watercolor brush to work the silica gel between the petals, as shown in **Diagram 3.**

Silica gel

End of water-color brush

Push silica gel particles between petals

DIAGRAM 3

I also work the silica gel between the flower petals by gently moving the container from side to side while keeping the bottom of it on the counter surface. Or you can pick up the container with one hand and gently tap it against the palm of your other hand. The flower should be well covered, but it's not necessary to fill the container completely. I then place a lid on the container and put a label on it that identifies the flower and indicates what day it was placed in the silica gel.

If I can choose to place a flower face up or face down on a bed of silica gel, I almost always place it face up. This way it will be easier to get the silica grains between the petals because I can gently push them in there if needed. The exception would be when I dry flowers shaped like Queen-Anne's-lace, coneflowers, verbena, or lilac, which have small flower heads made up of many individual soft-petaled florets, and larger flower heads of the same shape, such as mop-head hydrangeas. I find that it's much easier to keep the shape of these flowers if I hold them by the stems with the flower heads facing the bottom of the container and then begin to slowly pour silica gel down through them. If I place the blossoms in the container with the stem at the bottom, it takes too much time to make sure that I don't weigh down the tops of the blossoms with the silica gel, which would distort or flatten their shapes.

DRYING MULTIPLE FLOWERS IN THE SAME CONTAINER

If you've picked a bunch of flowers of the same type from your garden, it isn't necessary to place them in separate containers to dry. Simply follow the same basic procedure described in "Drying a Single Blossom" on page 23. Pour a bed of silica gel into the bottom of the container, arrange the blossoms in the particles so they are not touching each other, and begin to cover them with silica gel. I often use a funnel or a measuring cup to build up little mounds between each flower, making certain that the silica gel gets in between and up under all the petals.

If the container is deep enough, I'll add another layer of flowers. I make sure the first layer is completely covered, and then I repeat the process.

It is possible to place flowers of different varieties in the same container as well, but this gets a bit tricky. If you want to do this, choose flowers that have similar drying times (see "Flower Drying Timetable" on page 159).

DRYING FLOWERS WITH SPECIAL NEEDS

There are flowers that have presented particular challenges to me (such as lilies and flowers with long stalks). You can follow my guidelines when drying these flowers and others with similar shapes.

Lilies

Some parts of a flower are more dense and hold more water than other parts. Usually these parts are those that have to do with the flower's reproduction process and are in the center of the

When covering flowers for drying, I sometimes fill a funnel with silica gel and control the amount that flows out of the end of the funnel with my finger. This can be a good way to expedite the covering process.

flower or at the base where the petals are connected. This is true for lilies. What makes the drying process frustrating when working with lilies and other flowers like them is that each part of these flowers takes a different amount of time to dry. If left intact, lily petals are dry days before the pistils are, and lily petals can have one of the longest drying times of any flower!

To expedite a lily's drying process, I remove some of its dense center by carefully snipping out its pistil and stamen and placing them off to the side of the lily in the silica gel to dry. This way, when the lily is dry, these parts will be dry and can be hot-glued back in place. Sometimes it can be a little tricky to snip the reproductive parts loose without snipping the flower, especially on flowers like calla lilies, so be careful and don't hurry. I find that I'm most apt to break a flower petal or have some other accident happen when I hurry.

The pistils and stamen of a lily are very susceptible to moisture reabsorption and will droop at the least bit of humidity. Occasionally I replace them with a leaf stalk of a pinnate leaf, such as those from walnut or locust trees, as shown in **Diagram 4** on the opposite page.

I use yellow or green spray paint to even out the color of the stalk, and then set it aside. When the leaf is dry, I cut a piece of dried stalk 2½ to 3 inches long and hot-glue it into the center of the lily to serve as the stamen, as shown in **Diagram 5** on the opposite page. I then cut lengths from the remaining axis to serve as pistils, and I glue them in place around the new stamen.

To make the lily look its freshest, I put a very small amount of glue on the underside of the dried anthers, or the pollen-producing parts of the stamen, and I rest them on the tips of the stamen. This requires a steady hand and patience, but the result is rewarding.

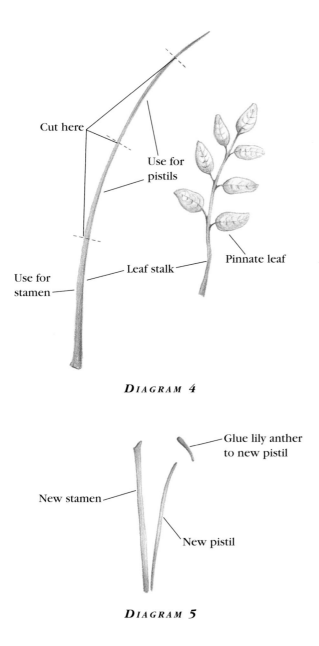

Cut here

Use for pistils

Pinnate leaf

Leaf stalk

Use for stamen

DIAGRAM 4

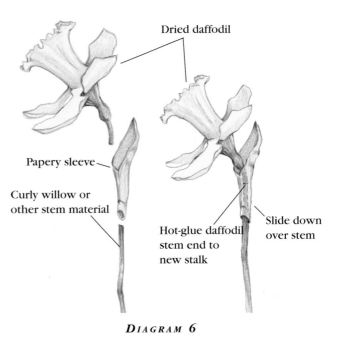

Glue lily anther to new pistil

New stamen

New pistil

DIAGRAM 5

If a lily is too big to fit in a container for drying, I gently break off individual petals, which I will reattach later, to trim the size of the lily until I can get it into the container, adding the loose petals and more silica gel, if needed, to the container.

If you have a lot of time and want to leave the entire lily intact to dry, it certainly can be done. But I'd suggest placing a small piece of a cardboard tube around the top of the pistil that extends up past the top edge of the petals. By using the piece of cardboard tube, you will be able to place silica gel around the pistil without filling the entire container, saving a good amount of silica gel.

To dry lily stems, I simply strip off their leaves, which have a tendency to brown when dried in silica gel, bunch them together, and hang them upside down to air-dry.

Daffodils

When I prepare a daffodil for drying, I like to snip it from its stem just below its ovary, as shown in **Diagram 6,** or the little bulbous part of the stem covered by a papery sheath. If, while doing this, I make the cut across the very bottom part of the sheath, I can then slide the sheath down and off the ovary and set it aside to put back on the dried daffodil. The ovary needs to remain intact or the pistils and stamen of the daffodil will fall out.

Dried daffodil

Papery sleeve

Curly willow or other stem material

Hot-glue daffodil stem end to new stalk

Slide down over stem

DIAGRAM 6

When the daffodil is dry and ready for use in an arrangement, I slide the sheath over the top of the stem material that will be attached to the flower, as shown on **Diagram 6** on page 27. I glue the daffodil to the top of the stem, and slide the sheath back in place. This makes for a realistic-looking daffodil, and the sheath hides the glued joint.

Flowers with Long Stalks

Tall, spiky flowers with individual blossoms that travel up and around the stock like delphinium, forsythia, and snapdragon present another challenge.

I dry delphinium on its side in a long, narrow box. Often, the individual delphinium spikes are longer than my boxes, so I simply cut them in two and insert a short wire up one of the stems so that the stem ends can be easily rejoined or reattached when dry (I use hot glue to do this). To make sure that I don't end up with a delphinium that comes out with a flat bottom side, I rest the stalks of the

When I dry spiky flowers like delphinium, I often support them on pieces of cardboard. This keeps the undersides of the flowers from resting on the bottom of the container and becoming flattened.

flower on little cardboard supports so they aren't lying flat against the bottom of the box. After the supports are in place, then I cover the flower with silica gel.

This technique doesn't work, however, with flower stalks that have cup-shaped flowers, because you can't get silica gel up into the cups on the side of the stalk that faces the bottom of the box. In a case like this, I snip all the blossoms from the flower stalk, dry them facing up, dry the stalk separately, and reattach the blossoms to the stalk with hot glue when all the pieces are dry.

Detaching and reattaching blossoms this way can be labor-intensive, but I'm willing to go to all that trouble because sometimes there is no other good drying method.

DRYING FOLIAGE

Whenever possible, I like to incorporate foliage into my dried arrangements. Foliage adds life to a piece and helps the piece look "real." Preserved foliage is especially nice and can be purchased at craft stores. Foliage dried in silica gel is lovely, too, and although it won't have the flexibility that preserved foliage will, it can still be used effectively.

Foliage is dried in the same way that flowers are—by being buried in silica gel. If the leaves have curves, make sure to preserve those curves when covering the leaves with the silica gel so the leaves don't come out flat. You'll want to allow time for the stalk or stem of the foliage to dry, too, and bear in mind that just because the leaves are dry doesn't mean the stem is dry. If the stem isn't dry, the petiole, or the little stem that holds the leaf to the main stem, will begin to droop, and the leaves on the stalk will look wilted. To test if a stem is dry, try snapping the stem. If it snaps crisply, it's a good indication of dryness.

When drying larger, individual leaves such as those that come from deciduous trees, a nice form can be retained if they are simply put between layers of newspapers to dry. This is an easy way to dry leaves that you may pick up in the fall. The weight of the newspaper alone (without any additional weight, such as books, placed on top) is enough to keep the leaves flat without making them look pressed. Without the newspapers, however, the leaves would curl.

USING HEAT TO DRY FLOWERS

I *often expedite drying times by placing drying flowers in a warm oven (80° to 90°F). The warm setting on gas ovens works well for this, but be careful with electric ovens because their warm settings usually are higher than these temperatures and are too hot to use. (The warm setting on my electric oven is 160°F.) A warm environment will cause a flower to lose its moisture more rapidly than a cool one. A hot environment, however, will burn a flower. You can also place covered containers of drying flowers in a warm attic. If you decide to speed up the drying process by using heat, monitor your flowers carefully.*

When you think of the quickest way to dry flowers, the microwave oven may be the first appliance that comes to mind. But when I tried it, what was supposed to have been a timesaving experience turned out to be a frustrating exercise.

I monitored the temperature, waited for the silica gel to cool, removed the flower, and found that it had not been heated enough to dry. So back in it went, or in some cases, I ended up throwing it away because in its only partially dry state, it was too limp to cover again with silica gel.

I don't want to discourage you from experimenting with your microwave oven if you wish, but I don't use it. My thinking is that some things, like cakes and flowers, are better off being heated elsewhere.

Determining When a Flower Is Dry

FLOWERS COME IN DIFFERENT SHAPES and sizes and with different densities to their petals. Additionally, the connecting tissues that hold the petals together, as well as the parts that the flower needs for reproduction, will vary in density from one flower to another. Some petals, like those of a magnolia, are very large and dense and contain a lot of moisture, while other petals, such as those of a dogwood (which is really a bract), contain

To test the dryness of a flower, I try to press my thumbnail into the flower's receptacle. If I can penetrate it, the flower isn't dry.

very little moisture. All of these factors determine how long a flower will take to dry. (See the "Flower Drying Timetable" on page 159 for drying times for different flowers.)

It is critical that the flower and all its connective tissue be completely dry when it is taken out of the silica gel, or it will wilt and fade. A test I use on roses is to see if my thumbnail will penetrate the flower's receptacle (to identify the receptacle, see **Diagram 1** on page 24). If it does, the flower isn't dry, and I place it back into a small amount of silica gel so that, at the very least, the receptacle is buried. It often isn't necessary to re-cover the whole flower, but on flowers with fairly dense center petals, such as a rose that isn't opened all the way, I figure that if the receptacle isn't dry, the rose probably isn't dry in the center either. I often grasp the petals of the rose that are still in bud form, and if they seem to have a little bit of give to them or feel a little spongy, it's important that they be re-covered as well. They will feel really crisp with no give at all when they are dry, and they will be lightweight.

Can flowers be too dry? The answer to this is yes. It may seem that since I'm concerned about drying blossoms, "too dry" would not be an issue. However, if flowers are left in silica gel for a period of time after they are dry, the petals on some flowers will detach when you pour off the silica gel, and some petals will become so brittle that they will break.

REMOVING FLOWERS FROM SILICA GEL

This is a process you don't want to hurry. You have been waiting for days to see if the flower you attempted to dry will turn out the way you had hoped, and it's easy to forget that dried flowers no longer have the flexibility they had when they were fresh. A hurried pouring off of silica gel can often irreparably break those lovely petals you have waited so long to reveal.

It's important to remember that dried flowers don't have nearly the give or flexibility of fresh ones, and if you grasp a dried flower too tightly, it's going to break, not give. You must develop a light touch when working with dried flowers—one that is firm enough to hold onto the flower or clean it off effectively, but only that. As often as possible, I handle flowers by their receptacles or bits of stem and not by their petals or centers. The less I handle the petals, the less likely I am to accidentally break them.

When removing a single flower from a container, I spread the fingers of one hand over the mouth of the container while I hold it with the other hand and slowly pour the silica gel onto a jelly roll pan, a cookie sheet with sides, or into a second container. A cookie sheet makes a nice receptacle for the silica gel because if the gel needs redrying, it will be ready to go into the oven. I keep the container I'm pouring from close to the cookie sheet to cut down on dust. With a larger container, I pour close to the box to soften the landing of the flower as it gets poured out. Silica gel is heavy, and if the flower is slowly "poured" out with the silica gel, it will fare far better than if it were to land with all the silica gel's weight rapidly pushing it from behind. I then pick up the flower by holding its stubby receptacle or stem.

Don't be tempted to rush when pouring off silica gel. Test the container on a cookie sheet and do it slowly. That way, the blossoms will not tumble out and break.

To remove multiple flowers that have been placed in the same container for drying, I stress again that you must pour off the silica gel *slowly*. You will have a lot of flowers to watch at once, and if you pour too quickly, it will cause them to tumble over themselves, and petals are apt to break off. I rest the container I'm pouring from on the cookie sheet and slowly begin to tip up the bottom of the container. As flowers become uncovered, I remove them with my fingers and set them aside.

There is a limit to the size of a container I'll use when drying a lot of flowers at once, because although I may be able to get a lot of flowers in a larger container, the bigger it is, the heavier it will get when filled with silica gel. When pouring off silica gel, it is a lot easier to control 5 pounds than 15 pounds.

Other Drying Mediums

ALTHOUGH I DRY all my flowers with silica gel, there are other drying mediums that are worth mentioning. Each has its advantages and drawbacks. You may want to experiment with several of these materials just to get a feel for them, but I think you will find that silica gel gives you the most consistent, desirable drying results.

SAND

The first flower I ever tried to dry came from my mother's rose garden. I dried it in sand that I had scooped up from nearby Douglas Creek. Much to my delight, the rose dried successfully, even though it had tiny indentations in the petals caused by the coarseness of the sand. I don't remember that this was a concern to me, however. I was just delighted that the flower had dried at all! Even with the availability of silica gel, sand is still a drying medium of choice for some flower dryers, and it can be a very effective one. But unlike silica gel, which has a unique set of unchanging characteristics, there are as many different kinds of sands as there are beaches and deserts on the earth.

Although sand is defined as particles formed from the breakdown of rocks and minerals, we tend to apply the term "sand" to anything that remotely resembles sand particles in appearance and size. Let me give you some examples. Some sands are formed from the breakdown of shells and corals. You could find these sands in the Bahamas. Oolitic sand, present in the Great Salt Lake, is formed not from a breaking down of something, but from a buildup of minerals around a smaller fragment. Still other sands may be evaporite deposits, or what is left behind when a lake with a high mineral content dries up or recedes. Sometimes sands that are formed in these ways are the best kind to use as flower-drying mediums because they are apt to be somewhat porous and smooth.

Sand is probably the oldest desiccant we know about. Natron, a salt that looks like sand grains and is found in parts of Africa, was used by the

All silica gel and dust particles must be cleaned from the petals of a dried flower. One way to do this is to pour sand over the petals.

Egyptians 3,000 years ago as a desiccant for mummification. Natron salts are porous precipitates of sodium carbonate and have an ability to absorb moisture and hold it. While other sands have varying degrees of that same ability, many others do not. Even though some sands may be somewhat porous, most—with the exception of a very few—don't have the drying abilities of silica gel.

If we talk about "true sands," however, or those that are formed from the breaking of rocks and minerals, we can detect unique differences among them. Like the rocks from which they were formed, some sands are very hard. These are typically the kinds of sands we find in the United States along the beaches of the mid- to upper Atlantic and Pacific coasts. They are quite often quartz sands. Other rocks that were formed largely from the buildup of organisms will erode into sands that are much softer and somewhat permeable, which means having some ability to absorb moisture.

Any sand, when exposed to continuous wind and wave action, will become worn and smooth over time, and the softer the sand, the more quickly this action takes place. If silica gel didn't exist and I were to choose an alternative flower-drying medium, sands of this type would be my choice.

The harder the rock from which the sand is formed, the less permeable the sand will be, and instead of drawing moisture into part of its internal structure, it attracts it to its surface. If a flower were to be buried in this type of sand for drying, the sand would attract the flower's moisture to the surface of the sand and to the dry little spaces between the grains, because the sand is dryer than the flower. Moisture would then escape from there out into the air, if the air were dryer than the sand. How the sand was formed determines its desiccating properties. If it has none, the weight of the sand will at least hold the flower in shape while it dries naturally.

ALTERNATIVE DRYING MEDIUMS

Before silica gel gained popularity as a drying agent for flowers, many other mediums, mixtures, and household products were used to dry flowers, with varying degrees of success. Among these were alum, plaster of Paris, cornstarch, baking soda, and a mixture of cornmeal and borax—which may be the one we are most familiar with. While many of these products had some desirable desiccating components, their biggest downfall was probably that, unlike silica gel or sand, they are all soluble in water to varying degrees, so as moisture was absorbed from a drying flower, the drying medium was apt to be altered and often changed from a granular or powdered form into a more solid form in places. Even still, flower dryers did enjoy good, if somewhat inconsistent, results with these different mediums. If you'd like to try some of these other products for flower drying, you may be able to find some older books in used bookstores or in your public library that could guide you.

If you decide to try sand as a drying medium, remember this: the softer the sand, the gentler it will be on your blossoms.

You can also use purchased sands. Pre-packaged sands have many different uses and therefore come in many different grades. If you decide to purchase sand to use for flower drying, I recommend trying those that are marked "play sand," which is usually made from crystalline silica.

Before using any sand as a dehydrating medium, whether it is gathered or purchased, wash it to remove any silt or residue. You may think that because sand is mined or gathered and packaged, it is ready to use; however, many unknown impurities will still be present that can interfere with the sand's ability to dry a flower.

To wash the sand, fill a bucket half full of sand and half full of warm water, add a small amount of liquid dish washing soap, and stir it up. Rinse the sand again and again (and again) until the rinse water is clear and free from soap. Then spread out the sand on a cookie sheet and place in a warm oven (approximately 250°F) to dry. Or spread the sand out to dry on a tarp or an old vinyl tablecloth that you've placed out in the sun. The sand will be ready to use when it is completely dry. If it looks as if the sand is a mixture of fine and coarse grains, sift it first. You'll want to use the finer sand particles because they will leave fewer indentations in the flower petals.

To dry a flower, choose a container that is close in size to the diameter of the flower so you don't have to use a larger amount of sand than necessary. Pour the sand into the container, and then place the flower in the sand so that the flower's stem and receptacle are buried. Then gently spoon sand around and between the petals of the flower, making sure the flower retains its original shape. You may need to pick up the container and gently tap it to distribute the sand between the petals. The flower should be well-covered, but the container does not have to be filled completely. Leave the container uncovered, and after a few days, check the flower to see if it has dried. When the flower is completely dried, remove it from the sand and gently brush off any remaining sand particles with a soft watercolor or cosmetic brush.

CAT-BOX LITTER

I hesitate to address something I've not actually tried, but I get a lot of questions about drying flowers in cat-box litter, so I think it's worth mentioning. A lot of granular cat-box litter is fuller's earth, a naturally occurring clay mineral. It is a composite of alumina, silica, iron oxides, lime, magnesia, and water in varying amounts, although the label will usually just say "clay." Although some of these minerals have dehydrating properties, others don't, and what is in the bag will largely depend on where the fuller's earth came from.

Cat-box litter is absorbent, as any of us with cats can attest to, and comes in varying degrees of coarseness, but bear in mind it is still *clay* and not sand. Although some brands are ground more finely than others, even the finest I could find was more coarse than any sand I would choose to use, and certainly more coarse than silica gel. Plus, I don't know what the "odor control" additive is and whether it will affect my flowers.

You may be tempted to try cat-box litter because it is much less expensive than silica gel, but remember that you're working with a medium that contains colorings and perfumes that you know nothing about, and there is no way you can be sure of the results you're going to achieve. However, if you feel like experimenting, by all means, try it. You may discover a brand that works well and does just what you had hoped it would!

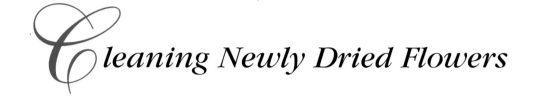Cleaning Newly Dried Flowers

WHEN I REMOVE DRIED FLOWERS from silica gel, they go right to my sandbox. No, not the backyard version for kids to play in, but rather a compact 12 × 12 × 9-inch box with about 4 inches of clean, small-grained play sand in it. I hold the newly dried flower over my sandbox and gently pour small amounts of sand over the petals to knock off the silica gel residue. I hold the flower up to good light and gently blow off any dust that may be clinging to the petals. Then I turn the flower upside down, and with my other hand, I gently bump it against the side of my thumb and

index finger where I'm holding the base of the flower. This knocks any embedded grains of sand or silica gel out of the flower's center. Or, while holding on to the flower's receptacle, I can gently tap it with the end of a small paintbrush while holding the flower upside down.

If I'm working with a lot of flowers (unless they're very delicate, like pansies, and susceptible to reabsorbing moisture), I often place them in sealed storage containers at this point and wait until I'm actually ready to use the flowers in an arrangement before doing the next step of fine-tuning. In the case of pansies, I thoroughly clean them before storing at this stage.

To fine-tune the cleaning, I use small water-color or cosmetic brushes to gently brush the petals while holding the flower by its receptacle and supporting the petals underneath with my fingers. If there isn't enough receptacle to get a good

After removing a flower from silica gel, I grasp the receptacle of the flower with one hand and slap it with the other hand to remove silica gel particles.

grip on it, I hot-glue a toothpick to the bottom of the flower to serve as a temporary stem. Cleaning can be a tedious process, but it's very important to do it thoroughly. Any silica gel residue left on the petals will give them a dull look and will attract moisture back to the petals—something you definitely want to avoid.

I often gently rub each petal between my thumb and index finger to feel how clean it is. Petals free of all silica gel dust will feel very smooth; those that still have some residue remaining on them will feel dusty. If any petals are loose or have fallen out during the uncovering process, this is the time to glue them back into the flower, and they can be reglued quite successfully with hot glue. If a petal seems to be loose, I pull it out and reglue it as well. Regluing one petal will usually benefit several other petals. I also like to put a drop of glue at the base of each outer petal where they join the receptacle. I often remove the sepals before doing this to achieve a better bond. (To identify the sepals, see **Diagram 1** on page 24.)

There are a lot of tricks I use to clean flowers. I often use a toothpick to flick clinging particles off individual flower petals.

There is one other cleaning technique that I use that can be quite helpful in some cases. When dealing with compound flowers, such as viburnum or lilac, that are made up of many small florets, cleaning with a brush can almost be more trouble than it's worth. And it seems that when I hold these flowers up to the light, I can always spot some twinkling grains of stubborn silica gel that are still clinging to petals. These grains will loosen if I pass the flower over a bit of steam and then tap the stem with a paintbrush handle to knock loose many of the remaining grains.

I clean the petals of flowers by dusting them individually with a soft watercolor or cosmetic brush.

Storing Dried Flowers

SOMETIMES, WHEN MY GARDEN is blooming, I find the drying process takes up so much of my time that the time I have to create arrangements is limited. The beauty of drying flowers is that they can be stored to use at a later date.

I like to store dried flowers in clear plastic 10 × 8 × 3-inch rectangular containers with clear lids. These containers stack well, and I can see at a glance what I have available when I'm looking for flowers to put into a specific floral piece. For larger flowers, I use larger clear plastic boxes, but these do not have clear lids, so I store them on a shelf where I can see into them from the sides. Many other types of containers will work for storage, as long as they are kept in a dry place or have lids that fit on them securely. I once used disposable containers with clear plastic lids from my grocery store's salad bar. Cookie and candy tins work well, too. You can use cardboard shoe boxes or any other cardboard box with a lid, but bear in mind that moisture can penetrate cardboard.

Regardless of what type of container I use for storing dried flowers, I always include a small open container of silica gel to ensure that the flowers will stay dry. I check the containers from time to time, especially during rainy periods, to make certain I can still see the blue indicators in the silica gel. If I can't, then I check the flower petals. If they feel less than crisp, I replace the silica gel with some that is dry. Floral spray paint lids make good containers for the silica gel.

HOW LONG WILL DRIED FLOWERS LAST?

Humidity and light are the two elements that rob a dried flower of its beauty more than anything else. Exposure to too much humidity will cause a flower to fade and wilt, while exposure to light by itself will cause a flower to fade over time. Therefore, how long a flower lasts—meaning the period of time when it will look the same as the day it came out of silica gel—will be determined by how much humidity and light it is exposed to over the course of its dried life.

Most dried flowers can tolerate a humidity level of 55 to 60 percent and still stay nice and crisp. In some parts of the country, humidity levels are much lower than that, while in other parts, like here in Virginia, humidity levels often exceed that.

The easiest way to provide an environment that's comfortable for dried flowers is to heat your home in the winter and to provide continuous air conditioning in the summer, both of which lower humidity levels. Or, you can run a dehumidifier. I monitor the humidity level constantly in my house using inexpensive humidity gauges, which are readily available in hardware or discount stores.

To extend the color life of a dried floral arrangement, keep it out of direct sunlight or bright indirect light. With proper care, a dried floral piece can last for years.

Modifying Dried Flowers

IT WOULD SEEM THAT once the flower is dry, the majority of work is done. In fact, it's actually just beginning. Before these beautifully dried specimens can be added to wreaths or arrangements, they often need modifying in order to retain their forms and colors. And if a flower is going into an arrangement, you will need to add a stem.

ADDING A STEM

Flowers that will be placed into arrangements obviously need to have stems added. But I also add stems to all the flowers that I place in my wreaths.

The stem allows me to work with the flower much more easily, and it gives me more options for placing the flower in the wreath.

Plain round toothpicks make great stems for single flowers going into wreaths. I simply glue one on to the back of the flower. I often add a toothpick before I fine-tune the cleaning (see "Cleaning Newly Dried Flowers" on page 35) because it gives me a way to hold the flower while I'm working with it. In addition, I can easily poke the flower into a piece of floral foam and keep it upright until I'm ready to use it. It's rare that these "stems" show when the flowers are in one

Before adding dried flowers to my arrangements, I often add stems to the blossoms, which allows me to work with the flower easily.

of my wreaths, but if I'm concerned that they may show, I color them with a green or brown felt-tip pen. If they extend past the back of the wreath, I clip them off.

Another option for adding a stem is to use any bits of leftover dried-flower stems, providing they are sturdy. I have a box containing stems that I use to attach to flower heads if I am going to use them in an arrangement. I use sturdy, air-dried stems, such as those from roses, and the bottom halves of long flower stems, such as larkspur, that I might have clipped off when I shortened them to use in arrangements. My box of stems contains stems that are pithy, such as those of coxcomb or papavar, and woody stems from various bushes and trees. Many, many stems will work well for this purpose, as long as they are sturdy.

Stems can be attached in several ways, depending on how "clean" the attachment needs to be and how much time you are willing to spend doing it.

The easiest and quickest way to attach a stem is simply to hot-glue it to the back of the flower. A small amount of glue may be visible when you do this, but it is on the back of the flower and generally can't be seen anyway. Prior to gluing a green stem to a flower, I usually spray it with green spray paint as close to its own color as I can get it, because it will fade. If it is a more woody type of stem, chances are it has already turned to a brown color, and spraying it green will make it come alive.

If you have gone to the trouble of placing short wires in the stems of flowers prior to placing them in silica gel, this is when it will pay off. Hollow or pithy stems, like larkspur or papavar, are ideal for wiring. Place a small amount of glue on the wire to hold it in the stem, and it will be undetectable. This will also give a clean look to the back of the flower.

I always snip flowers that I dry from their stems. Stems can be air-dried and reattached to a dried flower with hot glue. For wreaths, a natural looking stem is not needed and a toothpick can be substituted.

Another method for adding a stem is to glue it to the back of the flower and then wrap it with floral tape. Using green floral tape works well if you have a brown stem that you want to make green, but you don't want to paint it.

ADDING COLOR

If I'm going to add color to the flower, I do it at this point by lightly spraying it with the floral spray paints designed for this purpose. Yellows and greens are known to fade in flowers and foliage, so although the color of the flower or

CREATING STEMS FOR HEAVY MATERIALS

I find that it often helps to create a stem for heavy materials for extra reinforcement before adding them to a project. I make stems out of whatever sturdy materials I have lying around on my worktable, such as the ends of sturdy branches, pieces of miniature cattail stems, or wired stems taken off of commercially stemmed materials, like lotus pods.

When adding stems to artichokes and pomegranates, I first use an electric drill to drill a small hole in their bases. Then I cut a piece of stem material several inches long, coat one end with hot glue, and insert the stem end into the hole.

When I place the material in a wreath, for example, I then have the option of letting the item rest directly on the wreath base or allowing it to extend out a bit. By inserting the stem through the wreath base and gluing it in place, I find that the material will not fall out of the arrangement .

To make a stem for a pinecone, I cut a length of stem material and glue it directly to the base of the pinecone, placing glue in several places so the stem can't pop loose.

foliage may look vibrant when you remove it from the silica gel, I know that in a few months it won't. So I treat it with a color as close to its own as I can get.

To do this, cover your hand in a plastic bag, and hold the flower in that hand. Holding the can at least 12 to 16 inches away, begin to mist the flower. Paint slowly, building up the color gradually until it is the desired color. If you spray too quickly and too closely, the flower will look painted and shiny, a look I try to avoid.

SPRAY PAINTING LEAVES

Sometimes it's nice to add touches of gold to wreath material simply for interest or to create more of a holiday look. In "Backyard Gatherings" on page 132 I gave some salal leaves just a dusting of gold spray paint before I added them into the grapevine wreath, allowing some of the green of the salal leaves to show through the gold paint. By doing this, I created subtle touches of gold on this magnificent wreath instead of strong accents.

Leaves on a branch are always easier to spray than individual leaves. If some of the leaves are tightly bunched together on a branch, which would keep the paint from covering their fronts or backs, I hold the branch over a steaming teakettle and gently straighten out the leaves so their front surfaces will be better exposed to the spray paint. I flatten curled leaves by gently working them with my fingers, which is easily done once the leaves have been softened with the steam. Then I can spray paint the branch and every single leaf will be usable in my wreath or arrangement.

For a project involving a lot of dried leaves, I use leaves from my "leftover leaf box." Often these are individual leaves that are not attached to a stem. To paint these leaves, I insert the stem ends into a piece of the soft floral foam that is used as the base for fresh arrangements. I line the leaves up across the floral foam and around the sides—however I can place them so the paint will lightly cover the front and the back of each leaf.

APPLYING A SEALER

I spray all of my dried flowers with a sealer to help keep out moisture. Companies that cater to the floral industry have come up with a number of products that are sold specifically for this purpose. I have found that clear, satin acrylic sprays sold in craft or paint stores work well, too.

Bear in mind that no spray is absolutely going to keep any and all moisture out of dried flowers. (I still avoid placing silica gel-dried flower arrangements in a steamy bathroom, no matter what kind of sealer they have on them.) But my years of experience have shown me that some protection is better than none, and three coats are better than one.

Be sure to apply a sealer lightly to the petals, and spray them using a back and forth motion while holding the can at least 16 inches away from the petals. If you fail to do this, you may get a really shiny flower, even if you've used a satin finish spray. Experiment with the different types of sealers available, and choose your favorite.

No sealer—and I don't care what the can says—is going to keep a flower that is already losing its petals or dried material that is beginning to shatter from continuing to do so. A spray just isn't going to contain enough adhesive to keep that loss from progressing. A protective spray is just that, and it isn't designed to be a glue. If flowers are shattering, it's usually because they are too dry, too old, being tormented by an insect, or getting banged around and knocked loose by the opening and closing of a door. If you try to use a spray to correct those ills, you will be extremely disappointed.

Design
Basics

AFTER PUTTING IN HOURS OF WORK carefully harvesting and drying your flowers, you'll want to take the time to display them attractively. You may choose to create a wall decoration or a tabletop arrangement. Whichever you choose, remember that the manner in which you create a dried floral piece is just as important to consider as the care you give the flowers as you dry them.

In this chapter, I will give you tips on how to make and prepare wreath bases so they are sturdy and interesting, and I'll show you how to prepare containers and vases so they are ready to receive your exquisite dried flowers and foliage. Plus, I will give you design tips that will help you put your pieces together to form interesting and attractive decorations for your home or the homes of loved ones and friends.

Designing Wreaths

WHETHER I DESIGN a wreath using a twig base that will have a lush and abundant look to it when completed or a grapevine base that will hold a small collection of materials on one side, I choose materials from one of three groups of materials: key materials, primary fillers, and secondary fillers. Key materials are the star players of the piece. They set the tone for the wreath, and I choose them on the basis of the type and color of flower I use and the overall theme of the room or area in which I'll place the wreath. Primary fillers are flowers or materials that will complement or enhance the star players or key materials and that will tie the wreath together. Secondary fillers are those materials that serve as a backdrop for the other materials and fill in the base of the wreath. I always have a good idea of what each of these elements will be before I begin a wreath, and you should, too. It is important to have each element in a wreath work well with all of the other elements.

Although there are many different wreath bases available commercially and many types of materials that you can use to make your own bases, I find that two primary types of wreaths serve me well—wreath bases made from vines and those made from twigs. They can be added to or subtracted from quite easily, and they lend themselves nicely to my style of work.

When I create a vine wreath, I like to allow some of the vine to show through, adding interest to the piece.

VINE WREATHS

If you don't have a grapevine in your backyard, don't fret. Any vines or branches that are long and flexible and that can be formed into a circle without snapping will make a fine wreath base. At my farm, I have an abundance of vines to choose from—bittersweet, honeysuckle, trumpet vine, and Virginia creeper. They adorn the landscape more than I'd like them to, so I have a lot of material at hand. Fine, flexible branches from trees such as birch or willow also can be used to make lovely, interesting wreaths. While some less flexible materials, like pussy willow, can be used to form a wreath, you will sacrifice a lot of branches as they snap into pieces. Other branches, like those from weeping willows or birch trees, make absolutely lovely wreath bases and are quite easy to bend and shape.

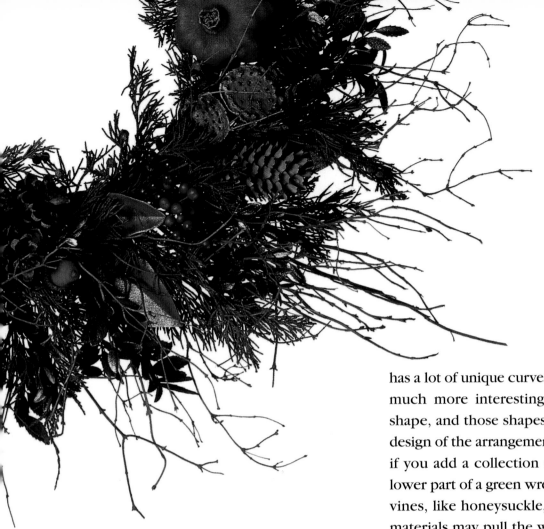

I've found that no matter what material I'm working with, it is easier to bend the vines into a wreath shape if I first cut the vine or branch to a manageable length. When I create a vine wreath, I sometimes wrap the vines inside a cardboard box so the wreath holds its shape. You can make your own wreath form by following the instructions in "Making a Wreath Form" on page 46.

How to Wrap a Vine Wreath

By wrapping your own vine wreath, you can make it the size you want it to be, and you can control its density by either wrapping it loosely or tightly. I prefer to wrap a vine wreath as loosely as I can and still have it retain its shape. A loose shape

has a lot of unique curves, hills, and valleys that are much more interesting than a tightly wrapped shape, and those shapes will help to enhance the design of the arrangement. Also, keep in mind that if you add a collection of heavy materials to the lower part of a green wreath made from less sturdy vines, like honeysuckle, the weight of the added materials may pull the wreath down, changing its shape from circular to oval.

When wrapping a vine wreath, it's easier to work with green, or fresh, materials. They are moist and flexible, and they're least likely to break or snap while you are forcing them into a circular shape. If a neighbor offers you grapevine that she pruned from her bushes weeks ago, and it is quite dry, try soaking it in your bathtub or leaving it out in the rain until it softens enough to work with without snapping.

Now, let's get started.

First, cut pieces of vine that are long enough to wrap around the circumference of the circle at least two to three times. This is a manageable length, and the wreath will hold together easily while you're wrapping it. If you cut a vine that is 15 to 20 feet long, you'll spend a lot of time pulling the vine through itself.

Making a Wreath Form

To make a wreath form, you'll need a bucket, tub, or round basket in which you will wrap the primary material. The form will contain the outside of the wreath, but to better control the inside circle of the wreath, you can place a small container inside a larger container—for example, a coffee can inside a round tub—and wrap the vine around the smaller form. If you are unwilling to give up any of your containers for a few weeks, or if you don't have any containers that are the size you need, you can make your own wreath form, using a square cardboard box. I have used a box measuring 14 × 14 × 5 inches. I cut pieces of cardboard from the flaps of the box that are 5 × 5 inches and glued them at an angle across the inside corners of the box, as shown, making the form inside the box somewhat octagonal. I then cut four more pieces of cardboard this same size and glued them to the bottom of the box, parallel to the first set and about 3½ inches in from the sides. I then laid the vine material between these pieces of cardboard to form the wreath.

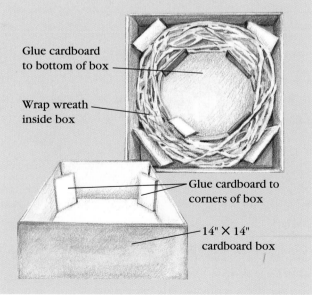

Glue cardboard to bottom of box

Wrap wreath inside box

Glue cardboard to corners of box

14" × 14" cardboard box

Second, grasp one end of the vine in your hand, and wrap the vine around to make a circle the desired size. Pull the free part of the vine through the inside of the circle, as shown in **Diagram 1,** and cross over the short tail of the vine to hold it in place. Continue weaving the vine in and out of the circle.

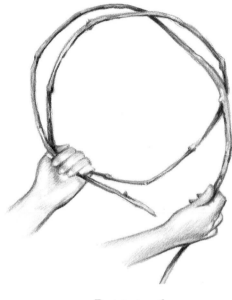

DIAGRAM 1

To add a new vine to the wreath, insert one end of the new vine between the natural gaps created between the pieces of vine, as shown in **Diagram 2** on the opposite page. Let that end extend outside the wreath if needed to keep it in place. The excess vine can be trimmed off later.

Continue adding and weaving vines in and out of the circle until the wreath is the desired thickness and size.

Before you add materials to the wreath base, always allow it to dry thoroughly. Hot glue adheres much better to dry material. Once the wreath form is dry, I use floral wire or hot glue to secure pieces of the vine together where they cross or overlap to help the wreath retain its form.

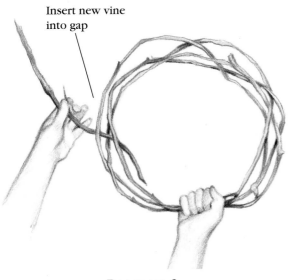

Insert new vine into gap

DIAGRAM 2

Using both floral wire and hot glue makes a very strong wreath. However, if a wreath is going to be hung on a wall with only relatively light-weight materials placed on it, there's no point in shoring it up as you would if it were going to host heavy items and be placed on a door.

HOW TO REDUCE THE DENSITY OF A GRAPEVINE WREATH

Many commercially made grapevine wreaths that are available in craft stores are made so they can be displayed unadorned or simply dressed up with a bow. If you choose to use one of these wreaths as a base for your dried materials, you may find that because the wreath is tight and dense, added materials will just lie on top of it and not really blend in with and become a part of the base. But you can loosen the wreath and rework it so it isn't so dense and tightly wound. Follow the steps below, and you may find that you can even make two wreaths out of one!

To separate a commercial grapevine wreath, cut any wire or cording holding the grapevine wreath together, as shown in **Diagram 3** on page

WHAT IS THE "WORKING CENTER"?

When I describe how to make many of the tabletop and wall pieces in this book, I use the term "working center." In wall pieces, this term refers to the point where the ends of stems, ribbons, and other key materials are glued and from which they radiate out—in other words, the point from which the piece is largely constructed. The working center is usually the focal point of the piece, as well. Occasionally, there can be more than one working center on a piece, in which case instructions will say "the working center in the upper left of the wreath," or I will define one as a "primary" working center and the other as a "secondary" working center, as shown.In tabletop pieces, the working center is also the point from which materials branch out. Again, it may not be the physical center of the container or piece, but it can be, and there can be more than one. In those cases, I will give you instructions so you can easily distinguish which center to work from.

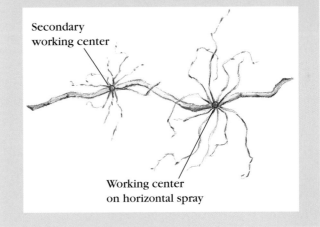

Secondary working center

Working center on horizontal spray

48. Then find the ends of the vines, and gently begin to pull the spiraled vines apart, as shown in **Diagram 4** on page 48, until the wreath is about half as thick as it was. Separate the section you have pulled from the wreath by cutting the vines

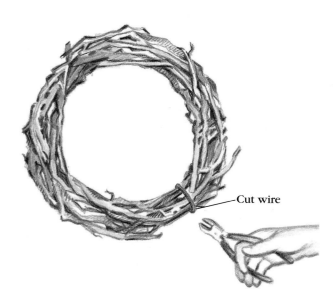

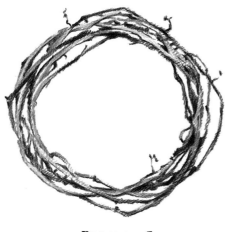

DIAGRAM 5

Cut wire

DIAGRAM 3

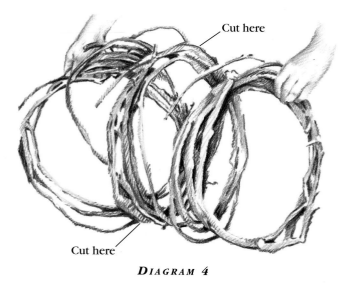

Cut here

Cut here

DIAGRAM 4

Enhance the wreath's design by gently pulling the vines up and out to create a pleasing shape with slight gaps between the vines.

When you have created a shape you like, secure it by tying together the vines that overlap with floral wire and putting hot glue on top of the wired joints. You'll get a better bond between two pieces of grapevine if you strip the skin away from

in several places, as shown in the diagram. Set aside one section of the vine. Some of the shorter pieces of vine that measure less than the circumference of the wreath may fall away from the vines when you do this. Set these aside to use later.

You will notice that the wreath you will be working with is already looser than it was, as shown in **Diagram 5.**

ADDING HEAVY MATERIALS TO ONLY ONE SIDE OF A WREATH

When you work with materials that have some physical weight to them, such as mossy sticks or branches, be aware that they may affect the way the wreath hangs. Too much weight added in one place will cause the wreath to hang off center.

This can be corrected if you counterbalance the weighty material with something else on the back of the wreath base. To add weight, hot-glue short, heavy sticks to the opposite side of the back of the completed wreath. Add just enough sticks for the wreath to hang correctly.

the vines at the places that are to be wired and glued together. The skin on a grapevine is often loose and may separate from the vine later, disrupting the bond. Work the ends of the vine down into the wreath so they blend into it.

If desired, add curved pieces of vine to the wreath, using the pieces of vine you set aside earlier to give it dimension, as shown in **Diagram 6.** If you need to give more of a curve to a piece of vine, steam it, as shown in "Bending with Steam" on page 50. I sometimes add more of these pieces to the wreath after most of the material is in place. That way I can get a better idea of where the added pieces will best enhance the shape of the wreath. Strip the skin from the vines, wire the vines together, and hot-glue them in place.

DIAGRAM 6

TWIG WREATHS

Twig wreaths provide a nice alternative base for wreath makers. These wreaths are composed of little groups of twigs bunched together and secured to a metal wreath form. Not only do the twigs help to hold filler material in place while the hot glue is drying, but they also extend out into

MAKING A GRAPEVINE ARCH

I often use grapevine that's left over from reducing the size of a wreath (see "How to Reduce the Density of a Grapevine Wreath" on page 47) to make the bases for grapevine arches. Just like my wreaths, when I create arches or sprays to use as bases for my arrangements, I want them to hold my materials in place, and I don't want them to be too fat or too heavy.

To make a grapevine arch, cut the leftover vines in half, select four or five pieces, and wire them together at their ends, as shown in the diagram. Make a wire hanger, securing it to the center of the arch.

Cut off any tendrils that are on the vine, and set them aside. If desired, you can hot-glue the tendrils to the arch to fill out the completed arrangement.

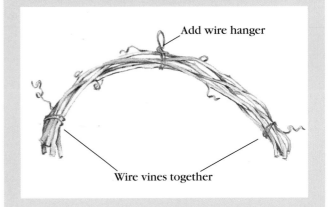

Add wire hanger

Wire vines together

the wreath itself and become part of the finished look. Like a vine wreath, a twig wreath also looks nice when it has a minimum of adornment.

While twig wreaths are not difficult to make, the process is time-consuming. Because they require a good deal of defoliated and often bud-bearing new-growth twigs, which I'm not eager to sacrifice, I usually purchase my twig wreath

Bending with Steam

Nature often gives us vines, twigs, or branches that don't come with the kind of curves we need in our design. We can spend hours looking for a twig or vine in just the right shape, or we can create that shape by using steam from a teakettle filled with boiling water. Once you have a good head of steam built up in a teakettle, hold the branch, twig, or vine over the steam with both hands (being careful not to place your hands in the path of the steam), and gently apply pressure to the ends of the material, gradually forcing it down in a curve. The steam will soften the material in the middle, allowing it to give and bend, and as you apply pressure, a curve will be created.

Don't prematurely force the branch or twig, or it will snap rather than bend. Older, drier materials, as well as thicker materials, take longer to soften than fresher or finer material. I also use this trick for bending flower stems, curly willow branches, or any other material that will be enhanced by a slight curve.

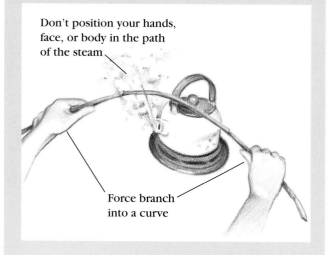

Don't position your hands, face, or body in the path of the steam

Force branch into a curve

While wrapping a vine wreath can be a relatively simple procedure, I save design time by purchasing a premade twig wreath base.

bases. If you choose to purchase a twig wreath base, you should be able to find one at your local craft store.

Commercial twig wreaths are made from wild shrubs or trees that are indigenous to different areas of the country. As a result, a lot of different twig wreaths, including huckleberry, mossy branch, quail brush, manzanita, and larch are available.

As with purchased grapevine wreaths, purchased twig wreaths are very full and dense, and before I do anything else to a twig wreath, I thin it out, removing up to half of the twig material. Because removing the material will loosen the wire holding the remaining material in place, the wire must be tightened so the material is again secure. If material is held in place by clamps, the clamps must be closed more tightly so that the twig material isn't loose. By thinning out the twigs, I can work the filler material between the remaining twigs.

How to Make a Twig Wreath

You may be fortunate to have bushes in your backyard from which you can harvest material to make twig wreaths, or you can use prunings or clippings from shrubs or trees. You may also live in an area where wild materials are available. Just remember, it takes a good deal of material to make a twig wreath. Make sure you are not selecting or cutting any endangered plant life.

Whether your materials are fresh or dry, the wreath is constructed on a wreath form. There are two types of forms that you can choose from: a wire box frame to which bunches of twigs are attached with wire, or a circular metal frame with wire extensions that you bend and clamp over the twig material, as shown in **Diagram 7.**

Whichever type of form you choose to use, you must first bundle the twigs together, as shown in **Diagram 7,** and either clamp the bundle to the wreath or secure it in place using 18-gauge wire. If the bundles of twigs are wired together as a bunch before they are placed on either form, they will be easier to handle, and you won't run the risk of their coming unbundled as you work with them. It will also give you an idea of how much material you actually have to work with. There is

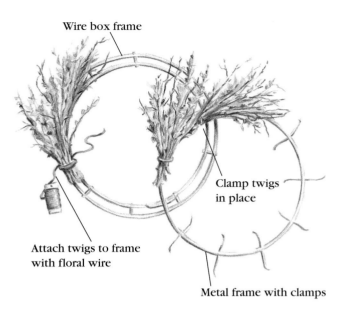

Wire box frame

Clamp twigs in place

Attach twigs to frame with floral wire

Metal frame with clamps

DIAGRAM 7

nothing more frustrating when making a twig wreath than running out of material before you finish the wreath! When assembling the bundles, combine stems of slightly different lengths in each bunch, so the material in the next bunch will lie flatter against the wreath form.

If you choose to use a wire form without clamps, you can either wire each bundle to the form separately, or you can leave the wire on its paddle and use one continuous length of wire as you work around the form, wrapping each bunch several times with the wire.

Designing Arrangements

WICKER BASKETS, CERAMIC, CLAY, wooden, or brass containers, or even glass jars or vases can all be used to hold dried-flower arrangements. Whatever container I choose, the mechanics of creating an arrangement are the same. I start by cutting a piece of floral foam so that it fits the container snugly and extends slightly above the top edge of the container, as shown in **Diagram 8.** This way, it will be easier to add material around the bottom of the arrangement.

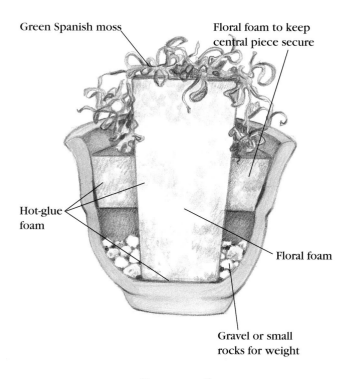

Green Spanish moss

Floral foam to keep central piece secure

Hot-glue foam

Floral foam

Gravel or small rocks for weight

DIAGRAM 8

I then hot-glue the foam to the bottom of the container. If you don't want to glue anything to the container, create the arrangement in a container that will fit inside the original container, or choose a different container altogether. You must secure the foam inside the container so it doesn't move out of position before you begin to make the arrangement.

I add weight to the arrangement by placing gravel or small rocks around the sides of the foam, as shown in **Diagram 8.** Dried arrangements, especially those made in baskets, are surprisingly light and can tip or be knocked over easily. It's best to save yourself some grief and give it an anchor right away by adding the rocks. If needed, cut smaller pieces of floral foam and wedge them securely between the central piece of foam and the sides of the container, hot-gluing them in place, as shown in **Diagram 8.**

Next, I cover the floral foam using green Spanish moss, as shown in **Diagram 8.** I use just enough moss to cover the foam, tucking it down around the sides between the foam and the inside of the container. If you use too much Spanish moss, it will be more difficult to insert material into the foam.

Arrangements made in tall or glass containers require slightly different methods of assembly. For instructions, see "Creating Arrangements in Tall Vases" on page 57 and "Springtime Masterpiece" on page 106.

Don't overlook items you have around your home. In my home I have a cabinet in which I store various sizes and shapes of containers. By keeping a stock of containers on hand, I always have a nice selection from which to choose.

DESIGNING A TABLETOP PIECE

Every floral designer has his or her own unique method of creating a tabletop floral arrangement. Often one begins by establishing the basic form or outline of the piece by inserting some key materials into the container, such as fo-liage, to establish that form. Other materials are then placed within the perimeter of that form, and the arrangement takes shape.

Working with dried materials, however, poses some unique situations that don't exist when dealing with fresh flowers. Dried flowers are fragile and inflexible. When I first began arranging dried materials, I found that if I accidentally brushed one dried flower against another while making an arrangement, a petal or two could get broken. If a flower had to be inserted between two others that were relatively close together, there might have been room for that flower and its stem, but not for my hand and fingers, which were needed to get the flower into place.

So now, when I make an arrangement, I start to work at the top center of the piece, as shown in **Diagram 9,** and move down and around the arrangement, establishing the form as I go. It took some practice before I was able to achieve the form that I had in my mind's eye, but it now comes easily.

When creating tabletop arrangements, I attach a separate stem to each dried flower. This allows me to make the stem the length I need it to be, as

well as to have it curve if desired. I can also position the flower head on the stem at the angle desired. As I go, I think about the juxtaposed textures, shapes, colors, sizes, and densities of each element, too. By always having a nice variety of dried materials when I start to create a tabletop arrangement, I know I will end up with a piece that has an interesting mix of elements.

After inserting all of the materials at the top center of the arrangement, I move down the piece, adding more dried materials, as shown in **Diagram 10.**

The last step is to insert greenery around the outside base of the arrangement, so that a leaf or two hangs down over the edge of the container, as shown in **Diagram 11.** This gives the piece some depth and covers the moss.

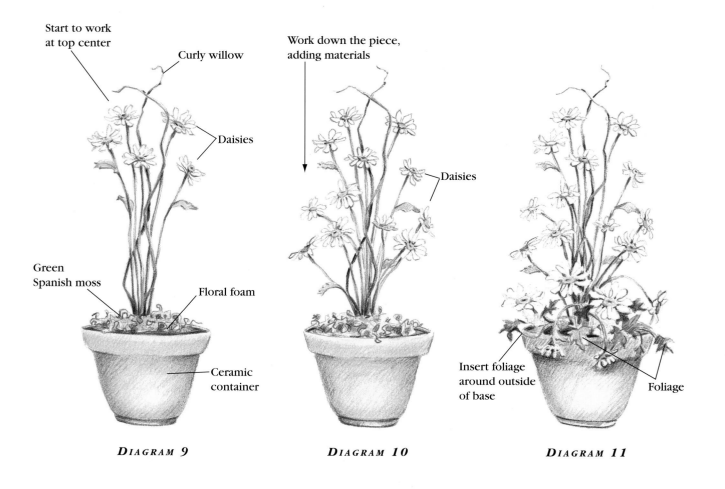

DIAGRAM 9 *DIAGRAM 10* *DIAGRAM 11*

Tips for Choosing *Floral Foam*

There are several types of floral foams on the market, and they all have different functions. They vary in density, permeability, and color, and most are manufactured to be compatible with high- or low-temperature glues. When you shop for foam, you must be aware of the hardness and permeability of each type. Some foams will easily accept the stem of a dried flower, while that same stem would break if you tried to insert it into a harder foam. Unfortunately, what each foam is primarily designed for isn't always on the package, so use the guidelines below when selecting floral foam, or ask a knowledgeable sales clerk for assistance in choosing the right foam.

Floral foams are sold in a variety of types, colors, and shapes.

- **Dark green floral foam** is designed for fresh flowers and is very soft and permeable. If it is bumped or gripped too hard in its dry state, it will be easily indented. This foam has the unique ability to absorb water and hold it, much like a sponge. The foam will accept high- or low-temperature glues without melting, but such glues applied to its surface don't adhere well and are easily peeled off.

- **Gray or light green floral foam** is slightly less permeable and is widely used for silk or dried-flower arrangements, as well as for a variety of craft projects. It can also be found in shades of green and is compatible with high- or low-temperature glues. It is most often used for the type of arrangements featured in this book.

- **White or light green foam** is sturdier and harder to penetrate. It will hold things like wooden picks well. If you want to be sure that items won't move around at all once inserted, this is the floral foam to use. This foam is often sold in sheets or formed pieces and can be glued successfully with high- or low-temperature glue. If it is shaped like a cone or a ball, its exterior is often smoothed.

- **Extruded foam** comes in a specific shape or form, such as for a wreath or topiary. It may have some internal support as well, and, although porous on the inside, it has a smooth, shiny, hard exterior and is usually green. High- or low-temperature glues can be used with this foam, and because it often has extra internal support, it is often used as a base for pieces that will be heavier when finished, such as pinecone wreaths.

Small arrangements or groupings, whether in little baskets with lids or in mugs or small containers, are constructed from the top down or the inside out. I do, however, construct low, flat, centerpiece arrangements from the outside in or from bottom to top. I make bridal bouquets working from the outside in, too, but I almost never establish a form first and then fill in. Experience has taught me that it just doesn't work well with dried flowers.

MAKING RIBBON LOOPS AND TAILS

I seldom make a single, solid bow and add it in its entirety to a dried floral arrangement. I like to control where the loops of a bow fall in a piece, and I find I can do this more easily if I make individual loops and tails and place them exactly where I want them. Often, I work them in between the dried materials and not just in one central area, creating the illusion of a bow. Plus, I save ribbon this way.

Because I want my ribbon loops to have a "gathered" look, as if they were part of a bow, I take a section of ribbon twice as long as the finished loop will be (for example, 4 inches for a 2-inch loop), fold the piece of ribbon in half, and bunch the ends tightly together with my fingers. I then wrap transparent tape around these ends, as shown, and I have a loop that is easy to glue anywhere I want it. I find transparent tape is a lot handier to use than floral wire and,

oddly enough, hot- or low-temperature glue won't melt the transparent tape. I also make ribbon tails in much the same way, just by bunching one end of the ribbon and taping it in place, as shown.

Some wreaths I make have the illusion of being wrapped all the way around with a length of ribbon, but, in fact, they are simply accented with pieces of ribbon that are extended between materials on the front surface. In this case, I decide where I want to place the ribbon in the dried arrangement, cut a section of ribbon slightly longer that the length I need it to be, tape both ends separately, and glue it in place. If it's slightly longer than the distance between the two points I glued it to, it doesn't lie so tight and flat, and if it is a wired ribbon, I can give it an interesting bend or two. This is really a ribbon saver!

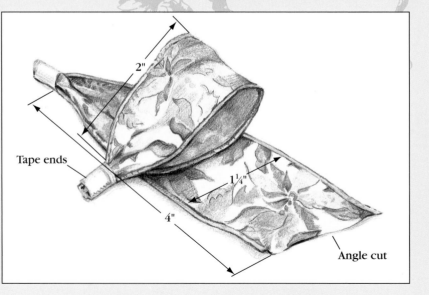

2"

Tape ends

1¼"

4"

Angle cut

CREATING ARRANGEMENTS IN TALL VASES

When I create arrangements in tall vases, I seldom add flower stems that are long enough to reach the bottom of the container because the stems won't be visible. (The exception to this is if I'm working with a glass vase where the stems will show.) This way, I not only save on stem material, but I also can simplify the mechanics for creating this type of an arrangement.

Although the stems are short, I always cut the block of foam to fit the entire depth of the vase, as shown.

I've found that if the floral foam does not extend to the bottom of the vase, the foam can break off as the stems are added, and the arrangement falls apart. Experience has taught me that it's best not to skimp on floral foam when I'm making larger arrangements.

If I don't have a piece of foam long enough, I extend the height of the foam by hot-gluing smaller blocks to the bottom of the main block, as shown, not the top. There are two reasons for doing this: A glued joint won't be as strong as a solid piece of foam, and you won't be able to insert any materials through the hardened hot glue. With the glued joint at the bottom, I have a nice, strong piece of floral foam at the top where I'll need it to do my work.

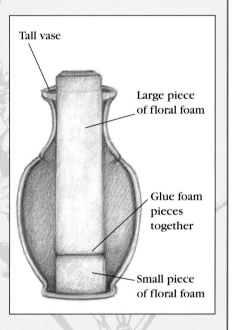

Tall vase

Large piece of floral foam

Glue foam pieces together

Small piece of floral foam

Lasting Mementos

A few cherished items have been passed down over the years by my grandmothers and mother. Because I'm a bit of a squirrel myself, I also have some treasures I've kept from my childhood. Most of the time these items are displayed in glass-front cabinets or are carefully stored in boxes, but on special occasions I like to display them more prominently, and I often add dried flowers for a colorful touch. Use the ideas in this chapter as a starting point for dressing up your own family heirlooms.

Remembrances

A shadow box is a charming way to preserve and display a collection of items commemorating a special occasion. Photographs, invitations, ribbons, and other memorabilia can be attractively arranged with flowers from the occasion to create something that can be enjoyed for years to come.

Commemorative items of your choice (I used a wedding invitation along with silica gel–dried and sealed flowers, plus ribbon from the wedding bouquet)

Preserved greenery (I used ivy and leatherleaf)

Lined shadow box at least 2 inches deep (2½ inches deep for larger flowers), with a removable back

¼-inch-thick foam core

Utility knife

Spray adhesive

Scissors or shears

Stiff paper or cardboard

Hot-glue gun and glue sticks

White craft glue

WHAT YOU DO

1. Mount the invitation on the foam core, trimming the excess foam core with the utility knife as needed, to raise the invitation up off the back of the shadow box. To mount the invitation, lightly spray the back of it with spray adhesive, following the manufacturer's instructions. Press the invitation into place on the foam core.

2. Use the scissors or shears to cut a piece of stiff paper or cardboard to the same size as the back of the shadow box. This will serve as a practice board for the final arrangement. Tentatively arrange the collection of items on the paper or cardboard as you would like them to appear in the finished piece. Place all of the items at least ½ inch in from the edges so that the materials won't get caught between the backing and the frame when the box is put back together. Measure the depth of the items as they are arranged, making sure they don't exceed the depth of the box.

3. Transfer the arrangement to the inside back of the shadow box. Since the flowers and other materials often overlap the invitation or photograph chosen for the center of the box, begin by hot-gluing the invitation in place.

4. Transfer the flowers and greenery from the practice paper to the inside back of the box, gluing the flowers in place first. Hot-glue the greenery in place behind the flowers. Use greenery to fill any spaces between the flowers.

When creating this arrangement to commemorate a wedding, you can make a bow out of the ribbon that came with the bouquet, if there is one, and hot-glue it in place before arranging the rest of the ribbon. Arrange the rest of the ribbon on the inside back of the shadow box, creating attractive curves so it flows nicely. Use the scissors to cut it to size, and glue it in place using a very small amount of white glue. If the ribbon doesn't have wired edges, you will have to place small weighted items on the ribbon in various places to hold the curves in place until the glue dries.

5. Make sure everything you glued in place is firmly affixed to the inside back of the shadow box and that the inside of the glass is clean before you put the box back together.

$\mathcal{A}$pple Blossom Festival

The two lusterware vases I used for this project belonged to my paternal grandmother and were the start of what turned out to be my small lusterware collection. The design on the vases just begged for them to be filled with apple blossoms.

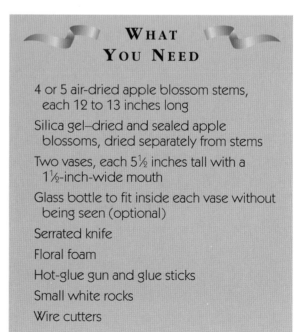

WHAT YOU NEED

4 or 5 air-dried apple blossom stems, each 12 to 13 inches long

Silica gel–dried and sealed apple blossoms, dried separately from stems

Two vases, each 5½ inches tall with a 1½-inch-wide mouth

Glass bottle to fit inside each vase without being seen (optional)

Serrated knife

Floral foam

Hot-glue gun and glue sticks

Small white rocks

Wire cutters

WHAT YOU DO

1. Insert a glass jar or bottle into each vase to hold the stem ends of the apple blossoms, if desired. The goal is to have the apple blossoms look as if they are coming out of a vase filled with water while keeping the mechanics out of sight. By placing the bottle inside the vase, you can achieve this effect without having to glue all of the materials directly into the vase. The mouth of the bottle should rest against the mouth of the vase; this will keep it from moving around inside the vase. If you have trouble finding a bottle that is tall enough, use the serrated knife to cut a small piece of floral foam, and place it in the vase underneath the bottle so it brings the mouth of the bottle up to the mouth of the vase. Hot-glue the foam to the bottom of the vase with a small amount of hot glue, and surround it with a few of the small white rocks for weight. Glue the bottom of the glass bottle to the floral foam.

2. Using the serrated knife, cut a small piece of floral foam about 1½ inches high that fits snugly inside the glass bottle. Push it down to the bottom of the bottle.

3. Use hot glue to reattach the apple blossoms to their stems. Carefully insert the stems into the floral foam inside the bottle; try to keep the stems from touching each other. To keep them from moving, place a small amount of hot glue on the stems where they rest against the edge of the glass.

DRY BLOSSOMS AND BRANCHES SEPARATELY

Since drying a whole branch of fruit blossoms would take an extremely large container, which I often don't have available, I dry the blossom clusters separately from the branches. Fruit blossoms are very delicate, and I find I have more control while covering and uncovering them with silica gel if I work with them separately. I snip the clusters of blossoms and their leaves from the main fruit branch. I air-dry the branches, and when the blossoms and the branches are dry, I reattach the blossom clusters to the branch. To help me remember how the branches and blossoms go together, I often take a photograph of the branch before I snip the blossoms from it.

Mirror Images

Small groupings of roses proved to be a nice accent for my grandfather's shaving mirror. The same arrangement can be used in several different ways. Add a bar pin back, and the roses can be worn on a hat or as a corsage. Add an elastic strap or hook-and-loop tape, and they become a wrist corsage.

WHAT YOU NEED

3 small, silica gel–dried and sealed
  roses

Small amount of preserved greenery
  (like a few ivy leaves or plumosus
  fern)

1 yard of green, wire-edged ribbon,
  1½ inches wide

Scissors or shears

¾ x 3¾-inch piece of mat board

Hot-glue gun and glue sticks

Wire cutters

Wrapped beading wire

WHAT YOU DO

1. Use the scissors to cut a 26-inch length of the wire-edged ribbon. Gather the ribbon on one side by grasping the wire in one hand and sliding the ribbon along the wire with the other hand, pushing it together from both ends. Continue to gather the ribbon until it measures about 8 inches, so that it fits around the outside edge of the mat board in an oval shape. Distribute the gathers evenly along the ribbon. Fold back the short edges of the ribbon, and glue them in place with a small amount of hot glue, overlapping the ends slightly so that the ribbon doesn't become ungathered. Using the wire cutters, trim off the excess wire. Hot-glue the gathered oval of ribbon to the mat board, as shown in the diagram.

2. Make a hanging loop with the beading wire, and glue it to the upper portion of the back side of the mat board.

3. Hot-glue the three roses in place, as shown in the photograph on the opposite page. Face the center rose straight up, but angle the other two roses slightly away from the center rose. Cut 2- to 2½-inch pieces of ribbon, and make small ribbon loops, following the instruc-

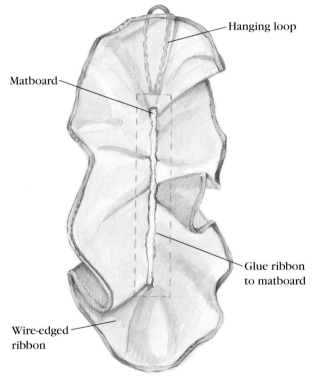

Hanging loop

Matboard

Glue ribbon
to matboard

Wire-edged
ribbon

HOT-GLUING RIBBON TO A MATBOARD

tions in "Making Ribbon Loops and Tails" on page 56, or make puffs to fill in the gaps between the roses. Hot-glue some ivy leaves or pieces of fern in and around the roses.

4. Using the hanging loop, display your arrangement.

Hidden Treasures

Flowers, ribbons, greenery, and a variety of other materials can turn the lids of baskets or boxes into colorful accents. The baskets also make lovely gifts, presented just as they are or filled with potpourri, a few tasty chocolates, or a small gift.

Tapestry and Roses

WHAT YOU NEED

2 silica gel–dried and sealed roses

1 medium dried artichoke

2 medium dried pomegranates

1 Norway spruce pinecone, 4 inches long

1 smaller red spruce pinecone

1 grouping of dried tetragonia pods, 4 inches long

3 honey locust pods with curls (can be any length)

1 dried golden mushroom, 3 to 4 inches across

8 to 10 green air-dried magnolia leaves

3 or 4 grapevine tendrils, 3 to 5 inches long

12-inch basket with lid

1⅝ yards of gold cord, ¼ inch in diameter

3-inch gold tassel

1⅛ yards of wire-edged tapestry ribbon, 3 inches wide

Toothpicks

Hot-glue gun and glue sticks

Scissors or shears

Wire cutters

WHAT YOU DO

1. Using the toothpicks, make short stems for the roses, artichoke, and pomegranates, if necessary, so that they can be hot-glued to the lid at an angle, using the diagram on page 69 for reference. (See "Adding a Stem" on page 38.)

Left to right: Tapestry and Roses, Winter Wonder, Sweetheart Basket, and Summer Fiesta.

2. Using hot glue, add the pinecones, tetragonia and locust pods, dried mushroom, magnolia leaves, and grapevine tendrils. Refer to the photograph above for placement of your materials, or experiment to see what looks best to you.

3. Prepare the ribbons as described in "Making Ribbon Loops and Tails" on page 56, and glue them to the piece. Cut and drape the cord and tassel attractively, using hot glue to secure them carefully to the arrangement.

Summer Fiesta

WHAT YOU NEED

4 silica gel–dried and sealed zinnias in assorted colors

2-inch sprig of silica gel–dried and sealed pepper berry

3 sprigs of silica gel–dried and sealed or air-dried goldenrod, 3 inches long

2 dried poppy pods with 1½-inch stems

6 green leaves, 2 inches long

7-inch basket with lid

24 inches of wire-edged ribbon, 1 inch wide

Toothpicks

Hot-glue gun and glue sticks

Wire cutters

WHAT YOU DO

1. Using the toothpicks, make short stems for the zinnias, following the instructions in "Adding a Stem" on page 38. Hot-glue them to the basket lid at an angle, using the diagram for reference.

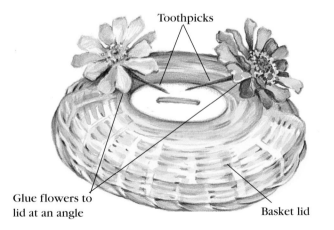

Toothpicks

Glue flowers to lid at an angle

Basket lid

HOT-GLUING THE MATERIALS TO THE BASKET LID

2. Using hot glue, add the sprigs of pepper berry and goldenrod, the poppy pods, and the leaves underneath the zinnias. As described in "Making Ribbon Loops and Tails" on page 56, prepare the ribbons and hot-glue them to the center of the arrangement, between the flower stems.

MAKE A BASKET TOP

If you don't want to hot-glue materials directly to a basket lid, make a top that can be attached to the basket temporarily. Because most dried material isn't going to be pretty forever, I like the option of being able to replace it on pieces like these baskets without damaging the basket lid. If I glue items to a little piece of cardboard I can tie onto the lid, I can simply untie it when I want to replace the basket decoration and start over.

Cut a circle of cardboard the same color as the basket. Using a utility knife, make two slits in the cardboard about ½ inch from the center and about ½ inch long. Slide a twist-tie through the slits so that the two ends are on the back side of the cardboard. Feed the ends through the wicker on the top of the basket, and tie them together on the inside of the lid. Hot-glue the flowers and materials to the cardboard circle.

Winter Wonder

WHAT YOU NEED

2 acorns

2 air-dried sprigs of rose hips, 1 to 2 inches long

1 hickory nut pod

2 grapevine tendrils sprayed gold

4 or 5 sprigs of preserved evergreen, 1 to 2½ inches long

4-inch basket with lid

12 inches of ribbon, ⅜ inch wide

Toothpicks or other stem material

Hot-glue gun and glue sticks

Wire cutters

WHAT YOU DO

1. Using the toothpicks, make short stems for the acorns and the hickory nut pod following the instructions in "Adding a Stem" on page 38. Hot-glue the acorns to the basket lid at an angle, using the diagram on the opposite page for reference.

2. Using hot glue, add the rose hips, hickory nut pod, grapevine tendrils, and evergreen pieces to the basket lid. Prepare the ribbon as described in "Making Ribbon Loops and Tails" on page 56, and glue the loops and tails to the arrangement, using the photo on page 67 for reference. Be careful not to overstuff the design, and keep in mind the size of the design in relation to the size of the basket.

Sweetheart Basket

WHAT YOU NEED

3 silica gel–dried and sealed roses in assorted colors

8 silica gel–dried and sealed fronds of bracken fern, 3 to 4 inches long, sprayed gold

3-inch cluster of dried berries, sprayed gold

10 to 12 leaves in different shades of green, 2 to 3 inches long

8-inch basket with lid

1⅛ yards of wire-edged ribbon, 2½ inches wide

Toothpicks

Hot-glue gun and glue sticks

Wire cutters

WHAT YOU DO

1. Using the toothpicks, make short stems for the roses, following the instructions in "Adding a Stem" on page 38, and hot-glue them to the basket lid at an angle, using the diagram on the opposite page for reference.

2. Using hot glue, add the bracken fern, berries, and leaves to the basket lid. Prepare the ribbon, as described in "Making Ribbon Loops and Tails" on page 56, and glue the ribbon loops and tails to the center of the basket lid, between the flower stems.

It *Starts* with a *Twig*

SOMETIMES THE SIMPLEST THING, like a twig, branch, or even a leaf, can spark a terrific idea for a wall arrangement or a table or mantel decoration. When you're walking on a woodland trail or taking a stroll through your neighborhood, allow yourself to appreciate the works of nature that lie in your path. Envision how these treasures could be used as a base for your dried flower arrangements.

Trail Mix

*Sometimes what makes a wreath interesting is its lack of perfectly
structured form. In this wreath, the free-form curly willow makes an ideal
base for a more wild-looking wreath. Use this photograph as a guide for
adding the other branches and materials, but do not limit yourself to the
materials I have used; work with some that are native to your area.*

WHAT YOU NEED

6 to 8 green curly willow branches, each at least 4 feet long

3 to 5 birch or larch branches, each 16 to 24 inches long

Several moss- or lichen-covered branches or sticks

6 to 8 fern fronds, each 4 to 8 inches long

2 stems of pitcher plant (*Sarracenia* spp.)*

3 poppy pods

1 dried hydrangea head

4 dried dogwood blossoms and a short dried dogwood branch

12 stems of air-dried ammobium blossoms

3 to 5 stems of dark green salal leaves, each about 5 inches long

Teakettle with boiling water

Hot-glue gun and glue sticks

Paddle floral wire

Toothpicks

**Pitcher plants are endangered
and should not be collected from
the wild. If you don't grow your
own, make sure that your floral
supplier is selling you propagated,
not wild-collected, plants.*

WHAT YOU DO

1. Bend the green curly willow branches into an oval shape to form the base for the wreath. You can create just the right shape by using a teakettle filled with boiling water (see "Bending with Steam" on page 50). Let the wreath shape dry for a few days before adding the other materials. That way, the dried materials will adhere better when they are glued in place.

2. Hot-glue the birch and mossy branches to the base to create a wild and somewhat messy look. The mossy branches are a little heavier than the other materials, so it's a good idea to wire them to the base in addition to hot-gluing them. (Before picking mosses in the wild, be sure none of them is an endangered species. If you are unsure, purchase moss from a reputable commercial source.)

3. Establish a working center at the lower right side of the wreath base (see "What Is the 'Working Center'?" on page 47). Working out from that center, hot-glue some fern fronds to the base so that they go up the right-hand side of the wreath. Add more ferns in the opposite direction so that they point down and across the bottom of the base at a slight angle.

4. Hot-glue the two pitcher plant stems, three poppy pods, and the hydrangea head to the working center, as shown in the photograph on page 72, or substitute your own dried materials.

5. Hot-glue three dried dogwood blossoms to a short dogwood branch, and glue the base of the branch to the wreath base on the upper left side, as shown in the photograph on page 72. Hot-glue the fourth dogwood blossom to a toothpick to create a stem, following the instructions in "Adding a Stem" on page 38. Then hot-glue the ends of the stems to the working center at the lower right side of the wreath base. Hot-glue some of the ammobium blossoms to this lower grouping.

6. Fill in behind both groupings of dried materials with ferns, ammobium blossoms, and salal leaves where needed for contrast and appearance. Individual curly willow branches, birch branches, or mossy branches can be added to the wreath at this point, too, until you achieve the desired look.

SECURING MATERIALS TO DOOR ARRANGEMENTS

Although a swag or wreath may have the appearance of being free-form, it still has to be solidly constructed, especially if it will be hung on a door. Because dried materials don't have the same flexibility as fresh materials, they don't tolerate motion as well, and you must make sure that every piece of material you glue to the piece won't move around.

The most solid area of the piece will be the working center, to which all of the dried elements will be glued (see "What Is the 'Working Center'?" on page 47). You will want to make stems for items like pinecones because unlike wire, rigid stems will keep the pinecones exactly in the place you intended. (For instructions, see "Creating Stems for Heavy Materials" on page 40.)

Some materials with a berry-like appearance, such as rose hips, seem to tolerate a good deal of motion. Others, like nandina, aren't so tolerant, and though it takes some time and effort, you may want to put a drop of glue at the base of each berry to secure it to the cluster.

When I hot-glue acorns to vines or branches, I make sure the acorns are securely affixed to their little "hats" and that the hats are secure on the branches. If an acorn is loose, I detach it and reglue it to the hat. If you gather up acorns when they are green, the natural "glue" that holds the hat to the base is at its sturdiest and seems to remain so throughout the life of the piece.

 Touch of Blue

This wall hanging was inspired by the wonderful, unpredictable shapes of the curly willow twigs and a desire to create a wall piece that wasn't a traditional wreath or horizontal wall spray. Since each curly willow twig has its own unique contours, every arrangement made from this wild-looking material is truly one of a kind.

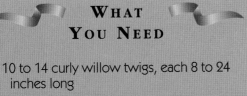

WHAT YOU NEED

10 to 14 curly willow twigs, each 8 to 24 inches long

6 to 10 stems of green preserved or air-dried salal leaves, each 10 to 14 inches long (how many you use will depend on how dense the leaf pattern is on each stem)

3 silica gel–dried and sealed stems of burgundy amaranthus, one 14, one 12, and one 6 inches long

2 silica gel–dried and sealed stems of pink astilbe, one 8 and one 12 inches long

1 burgundy and 2 deep pink air-dried roses with stems, each 8 to 24 inches long

5 air-dried blue hydrangea heads

1 burgundy, 1 lavender, and 1 light pink silica gel–dried and sealed rose

1¼ yards of woven tapestry wire-edged ribbon, 2 to 3 inches wide

Hot-glue gun and glue sticks

Paddle floral wire

Wire cutters

Scissors or shears

Ruler

Transparent tape

WHAT YOU DO

1. Make a base for the wall hanging by hot-gluing the curly willow twigs together, creating a working center, as shown in **Diagram 1.** (For instructions, see "What Is the 'Working Center'?" on page 47.) Take your time and work with the unique curves of the curly willow twigs to establish a loose, free-form arrangement. Reserve a few of the curly willow twigs to use as stem material for the flowers.

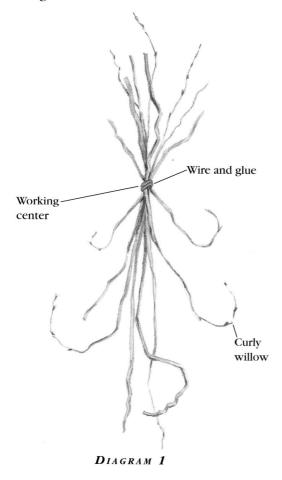

Wire and glue

Working
center

Curly
willow

D IAGRAM 1

2. Using the paddle floral wire, make a hanger and wire it to the back of the working center of the arrangement.

3. Hot-glue the salal stems to the curly willow base, as shown in **Diagram 2.**

Glue salal stems
to the curly
willow base

D IAGRAM 2

4. Use the scissors to cut a 24-inch piece of the woven tapestry wire-edged ribbon. Gather and tape one end of the ribbon, and cut the other end at an angle. Glue the taped end of the ribbon to the working center of the arrangement, and curve the ribbon down and over the curly willow twigs and salal leaves, as shown in **Diagram 3** on the opposite page, bending the wire in the ribbon to create unique twists and turns. Following the instructions in "Making

Ribbon Loops and Tails" on page 56, cut two 8-inch pieces of ribbon, and make two 4-inch loops. Make one 4-inch ribbon tail. Hot-glue the loops and tail in place, as shown in **Diagram 3**.

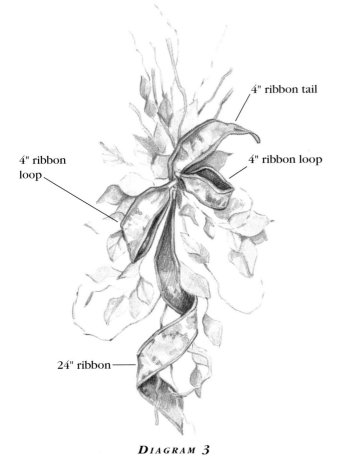

4" ribbon tail

4" ribbon loop

4" ribbon loop

24" ribbon

DIAGRAM 3

5. Using the photograph on page 75 as a guide for placement, glue the stems of amaranthus, astilbe, and the two deep pink air-dried roses to the working center of the wall hanging.

6. Make stems for the hydrangea heads from pieces of curly willow, following the instructions in "Adding a Stem" on page 38. Hot-glue the stem ends to the working center of the piece, using the photograph on page 75 as a guide for placement.

7. Make stems for the three silica gel–dried roses from the curly willow twigs. (The stem for the light pink rose in this arrangement is about 4 inches long.) Hot-glue the roses to the working center of the wall hanging, using the photograph on page 75 as a guide for placement.

8. Hot-glue the air-dried burgundy rose to the right of the silica gel–dried burgundy and lavender roses, as shown in the photograph on page 75.

9. If you want to give the top of the arrangement more fullness, cut and hot-glue additional curly willow twigs to the top of the arrangement, going up from the working center.

REARRANGING THE LEAVES

Sometimes when adding a branch of preserved leaves to a piece, some of the leaves may fall at an angle that doesn't enhance the piece much. When this occurs, I simply snip off a leaf here and there and reglue it back to the branch to give it a more pleasing angle or position.

$\mathcal{T}$wists and Turns

The curving lines and open spaces between the curly willow branches keep the eye moving around this rich-colored spray. Make your arrangement interesting by leaving those lines and spaces uncovered.

WHAT YOU NEED

24-inch-long curly willow branch, about ½ inch thick

4 to 6 finer curly willow branches, each about the same length (length can vary)

8 to 10 sprigs of preserved ivy, each 6 to 14 inches long

4 coral silica gel–dried and sealed zinnias (size can vary)

3 small yellow silica gel–dried and sealed zinnias

5 to 7 silica gel–dried and sealed

stems of purple larkspur, each 4 to 8 inches long

1⅓ yards of variegated blue wire-edged ribbon, 1½ inches wide

Teakettle with boiling water (optional)

Green 30-gauge wrapped beading wire

Hot-glue gun and glue sticks

Toothpicks

Scissors or shears

Wire cutters

the base will be sturdy. Form one or more wire loop hangers on the back of the curly willow base, as shown in the diagram.

2. Lay the pieces of ivy over the willow base in a pleasing arrangement, and wire and hot-glue them into place where they touch or cross over the willow. Lay the ribbon onto the base and the ivy, creating interesting curves and spaces as you arrange it. Wire the ribbon to the branches where they intersect, and hot-glue the ribbon in place.

3. Create stems for the larger zinnias using the toothpicks and following the instructions in "Adding a Stem" on page 38. Establish a focal point for the arrangement, and hot-glue the zinnias to that area, using the photograph as a guide for placement. To make some of the smaller zinnias appear to float, as I did, use pieces of curly willow for their stems if the toothpicks aren't long enough.

4. Glue the stems of dried and sealed purple larkspur behind the zinnias, keeping in mind the form you want the finished arrangement to take. For an eye-catching arrangement, you want the individual curves and curls of the willow to show as well as the spaces created by the looping ribbon. To do this, place the flowers so they enhance those shapes. If the ivy looks too dense, cut off a few leaves on the finished piece.

WHAT YOU DO

1. Examine the curly willow branches. If the finer branches aren't curly enough for your taste, follow the instructions in "Bending with Steam" on page 50, and use steam from a teakettle to gently create new curves in the branches. Once that is done, lay the finer pieces of curly willow down over the heavier branches until you have an interesting base for your arrangement, as shown. Wire the pieces of curly willow together where they intersect, and hot-glue them in place to ensure that

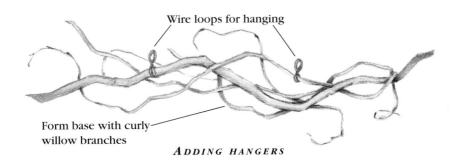

Wire loops for hanging

Form base with curly willow branches

ADDING HANGERS

Wildwood Flowers

Dogwood blossoms are some of the quickest and easiest little blossoms to dry. Because these sturdy white flowers actually dry white, they are stunning when massed together on a dogwood branch.

WHAT YOU NEED

60 to 75 silica gel–dried and sealed dogwood blossoms

4 air-dried dogwood branches, 12 to 14 inches long

Ceramic pitcher or other type of container (I used a pitcher that was 6½ inches tall with a 3½-inch mouth)

Glass jar or other type of container to fit down inside the pitcher (optional)

Teakettle with boiling water

Green 30-gauge wrapped beading wire

Wire cutters

Serrated knife

Floral foam

Hot-glue gun and glue sticks

WHAT YOU DO

1. Following the instructions in "Bending with Steam" on page 50, bend the dogwood branches so their tips are facing up. Hold each branch in this position until it dries, or tie beading wire to each end of the branch to hold the shape, as shown in the diagram. Wait until a branch has completely dried before working with it; otherwise you may lose the newly established curve as the branch dries.

2. If you don't want to hot-glue the branches directly to the bottom of the pitcher or other type of container, insert a glass jar that is no taller than the pitcher and whose mouth is close in size to the opening of the pitcher. Using the serrated knife, cut a 1-inch-tall block of floral foam, and place it snugly in the bottom of the glass jar to serve as an anchor for the base of the stems and to help stabilize the dogwood branches. If your hand is too large to fit down inside the glass jar, insert the tip of the serrated knife into the floral foam, and then lower it down into the bottom of the jar.

3. Use the wire cutters to cut the bottoms of the dogwood branches at an angle to make it easier to insert them into the floral foam. Then cut the branches to different lengths, which will make for an attractive display coming out of the container, and stick them into the floral foam so they radiate out from the pitcher or container.

4. Hot-glue the dogwood blossoms to the ends of the branches, using just enough glue to hold them in place. Since the branches are already in position, you won't break off flower petals when you position the branches as you would have if you'd glued the blossoms first and then positioned the branches.

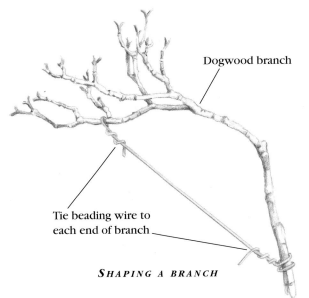

Dogwood branch

Tie beading wire to each end of branch

SHAPING A BRANCH

Tabletop Topiary Twins

*When creating my dried-flower arrangements, I stash away
any leftover materials that I may be able to use at a later date. These
stunning topiaries were the result of an accumulation of various types
of air-dried leaves left over from other projects. One nice feature of these
pieces is that the variety of leaves makes for more interesting topiaries.
I used a combination of bay, salal, diamond eucalyptus, tetragonia, and
oak leaves, but you can use leaves picked from your backyard.*

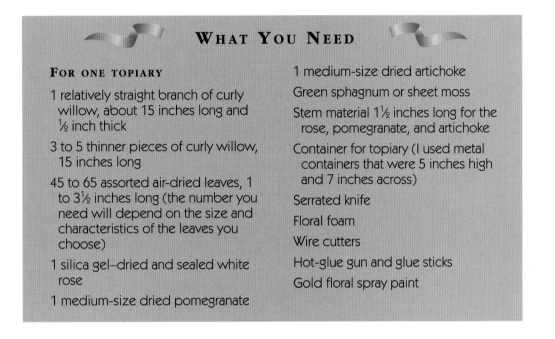

WHAT YOU NEED

FOR ONE TOPIARY

1 relatively straight branch of curly willow, about 15 inches long and ½ inch thick

3 to 5 thinner pieces of curly willow, 15 inches long

45 to 65 assorted air-dried leaves, 1 to 3½ inches long (the number you need will depend on the size and characteristics of the leaves you choose)

1 silica gel–dried and sealed white rose

1 medium-size dried pomegranate

1 medium-size dried artichoke

Green sphagnum or sheet moss

Stem material 1½ inches long for the rose, pomegranate, and artichoke

Container for topiary (I used metal containers that were 5 inches high and 7 inches across)

Serrated knife

Floral foam

Wire cutters

Hot-glue gun and glue sticks

Gold floral spray paint

WHAT YOU DO

1. Use the serrated knife to cut a piece of floral foam to fill the container and extend above the rim by about ½ inch. Hot-glue the foam to the inside of the container in several places so it won't wiggle around. Cut the remaining piece of floral foam to 3 × 4 × 4 inches. This will be the base for the topiary ball. (One block of floral foam was sufficient for the topiary shown, but if the container you choose to use is larger, you may need more.)

2. Use the wire cutters to cut the ends of the 15-inch pieces of curly willow at an angle, which will allow the branches to be easily inserted into the floral foam. Insert the thickest piece of curly willow about 2 inches deep into the center of the floral foam in the container, as shown in the diagram on page 84. Insert the remaining pieces of the curly willow into the foam around it. Center one of the 3-inch sides of the remaining piece of floral foam over the top of the willow pieces, and press the foam down over the willow pieces until the branches are about 2 inches into the foam. Place small amounts of hot glue at the base of the willow branches where they are inserted into the floral foam (top and bottom) to hold them in place. (You could cover the ends of the willow branches with hot glue before inserting them into the foam, but I sometimes want to reposition the floral foam, straighten the willow branches, or make minor adjustments to the arrangement, so I apply the hot glue later.)

3. Carefully insert the stem ends of the leaves into the top piece of floral foam, starting at the

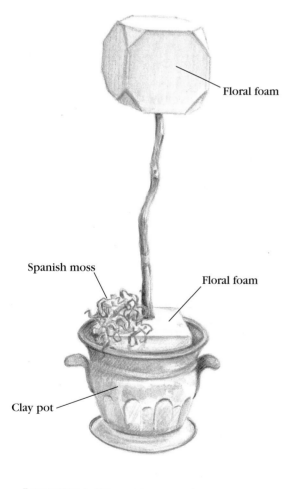

Floral foam

Spanish moss

Floral foam

Clay pot

INSERTING THE BRANCH INTO THE FOAM

center top and working your way down and around the foam. Since the floral foam used to make the topiary ball isn't equally wide on all sides, I round out the shape as I insert the leaves, using longer ones on the 4-inch sides and shorter ones on the 3-inch sides. If you have trouble inserting the leaves into floral foam made for dry materials without the ends of the leaves breaking off, purchase floral foam designed for use with fresh materials. Because this foam is much softer, it will be easier to insert the leaves. I like to use foam that is a little stiffer, however, because it holds the leaves better once they are inserted. If desired, you can always put a dab of hot glue on the stem end of the leaves before you insert them into the foam, but I find that this isn't essential as long as the topiary doesn't get bumped.

4. When the topiary ball is complete, I wrap a paper towel around the trunk to mask it, and then lightly spray the ball with gold spray paint. I like to just tint the leaves. Letting the different colors of the leaves show through the tint adds a nice antique feel. At the same time, lightly spray the rose, artichoke, and pomegranate.

5. Cover the floral foam at the base of the topiary with the moss, using hot-glue to hold it in place. (Before picking mosses in the wild, make sure none of them is an endangered species. If you are unsure, purchase moss from a reputable commercial source.) Make stems for the pomegranate, rose, and artichoke, following the instructions in "Adding a Stem" on page 38, and insert the stems into the floral foam at the base of the curly willow trunk. Insert a few leaves into the foam around the pomegranate, rose, and artichoke, as shown in the photograph on page 82.

Garden Party

*I found a half-dozen of these little crocheted baskets tucked away inside
a cigar box. Lined with colorful paper baking cups, they are the perfect
accent for a table set for tea, and little cups like these make nice favors for
my guests to take home. To add to the table setting, I arranged a delicate
grouping of pansies in an antique cream pitcher.*

WHAT YOU NEED

FOR ONE BASKET:

A cluster of 8 to 10 silica gel–dried
   pachysandra leaves, 1 to 1½ inches tall

6 to 8 silica gel–dried pansies in
   assorted colors

Curly willow branches

Crocheted and starched basket

Flat curtain weight, 1 inch across

Paper baking cup

Serrated knife

Floral foam

Green floral spray paint

Hot-glue gun and glue sticks

Scissors or shears

Wire cutters

WHAT YOU DO

1. Place the baking cup inside the basket. Using the knife, cut a piece of floral foam to fit inside the baking cup. Spray the floral foam with the green floral paint. When the paint is dry, hot-glue one side of the curtain weight to the bottom of the floral foam, and glue the other side of the weight to the bottom of the baking cup. By gluing the curtain weight to the bottom of the baking cup, you will add weight and stability to an otherwise very lightweight and top-heavy dried floral arrangement.

2. Hot-glue the cluster of dried pachysandra leaves into the center of the floral foam so that the leaves extend over the edge of the crocheted basket.

3. With curly willow, make stems for the pansies, as described in "Adding a Stem" on page 38, cutting the stem material to different lengths. Hot-glue one end of a stem to the back of each pansy. Cut the other end of the stem on an angle and insert it into the center of the foam between the leaves.

Curly Willow Corner Spray

If you let it, nature can help you with your designs. I followed the lead of the curly willow branches and the greenery in designing this piece, letting the natural materials wander along the pieces of molding that framed the doorway. Because I wanted to emphasize a wispy, natural look, I kept everything else I added to a minimum.

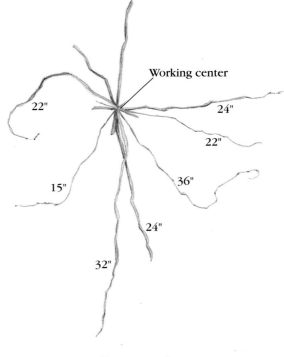

WHAT YOU NEED

7 to 10 pieces of curly willow or another curvy branch or vine, each 15 to 36 inches long

12 to 15 stems of preserved or silica gel–dried and sealed leafy greenery, each 5 to 24 inches long (I used spirea)

3 silica gel–dried and sealed pink roses

25 air-dried pink rosebuds

Hot-glue gun and glue sticks

Paddle floral wire

Wire cutters

Toothpicks

DIAGRAM 1

WHAT YOU DO

1. Create a base from the curly willow, using **Diagram 1** as a guide to length and placement of the pieces. Glue each piece of curly willow to the working center, letting the willow pieces overlap each other, and hot-glue them where they overlap. (See "What Is the 'Working Center'?" on page 47.) Each piece of willow and greenery is going to have unique curves and twists. Work with the individual characteristics of the material you are using.

2. Wrap the paddle floral wire around the base, and make a wire hanging loop at the working center of the wall hanging.

3. Add the spirea to the curly willow base, using **Diagram 2** as a guide for stem length and placement. Use the wire cutters to cut the tooth-picks to 1½ inches long, and hot-glue them to the bottom of the air-dried pink rosebuds, following the instructions in "Adding a Stem" on page 38. Hot-glue the flowers to the curly willow or spirea at the working center.

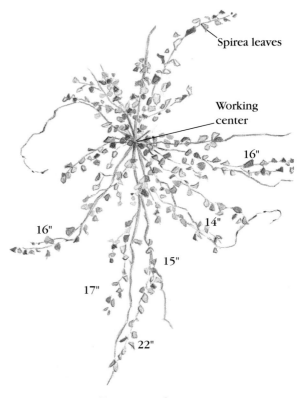

DIAGRAM 2

$\mathscr{W}$oodland Garden

Rustic-looking pieces like this woodsy basket are good ways to display some of these treasures you've picked up in your travels through the forest or by a pond. Don't limit your design to what you see here. Let your imagination run wild!

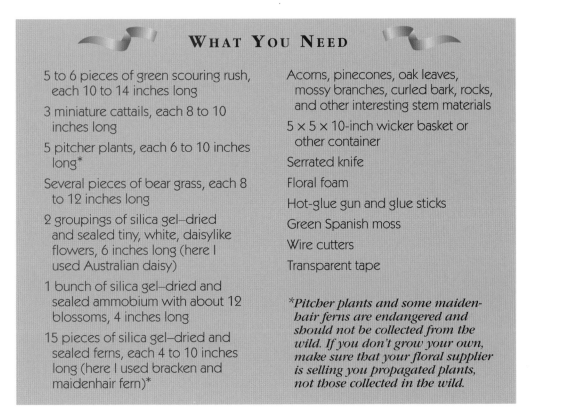

WHAT YOU NEED

5 to 6 pieces of green scouring rush, each 10 to 14 inches long

3 miniature cattails, each 8 to 10 inches long

5 pitcher plants, each 6 to 10 inches long*

Several pieces of bear grass, each 8 to 12 inches long

2 groupings of silica gel–dried and sealed tiny, white, daisylike flowers, 6 inches long (here I used Australian daisy)

1 bunch of silica gel–dried and sealed ammobium with about 12 blossoms, 4 inches long

15 pieces of silica gel–dried and sealed ferns, each 4 to 10 inches long (here I used bracken and maidenhair fern)*

Acorns, pinecones, oak leaves, mossy branches, curled bark, rocks, and other interesting stem materials

5 × 5 × 10-inch wicker basket or other container

Serrated knife

Floral foam

Hot-glue gun and glue sticks

Green Spanish moss

Wire cutters

Transparent tape

*Pitcher plants and some maidenhair ferns are endangered and should not be collected from the wild. If you don't grow your own, make sure that your floral supplier is selling you propagated plants, not those collected in the wild.

WHAT YOU DO

1. Using the serrated knife, cut the floral foam to fit inside the basket. Hot-glue the foam into the basket, and cover the foam with the Spanish moss.

2. You must add stems to the hollow stems of the rush and pitcher plants so you will be able to insert those materials into the floral foam. To do this, you can attach stems, or you can make your own stems from some of the cattail stems. To make stems from the cattails, cut the cattails to the length that you want them to be, and then cut the leftover stems into 2-inch-long pieces. When you are ready to place the rush and pitcher plants into the piece, cut them to the length you want them to be. Then apply hot glue to one end of each 2-inch cattail piece, and slide that end up into the hollow ends of the rush and pitcher plants about 1 inch, as shown in **Diagram 1.** Cut the other end of the cattail stem on an angle, and you'll have a nice, sturdy way to hold hollow-ended materials in place.

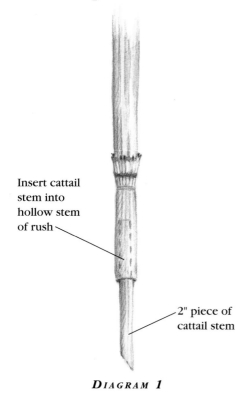

Insert cattail stem into hollow stem of rush

2" piece of cattail stem

DIAGRAM 1

3. Using the photograph on page 88 as a guide, insert the rush, pitcher plants, and cattails into the floral foam. Glue pieces of bear grass to the bases of the rushes and cattails. Insert stems of the miniature daisies into the foam next to the pitcher plants and rush groupings.

4. Create a small grouping of ammobium stems around one of the cattail stems, and tape them as shown in **Diagram 2.** Insert the ammobium stems into the arrangement, as shown in the photograph on page 88.

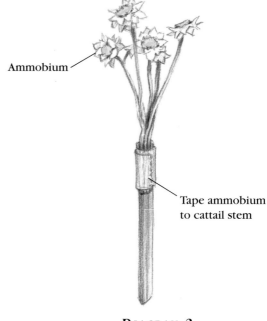

Ammobium

Tape ammobium to cattail stem

DIAGRAM 2

5. I found a curled piece of heavy bark that resembled a small hollow log, and I glued this to the floral foam at an angle between the two vertical groupings. I also glued a cattail stem to the back of a rock and inserted this into the floral foam to the front left of the pitcher plant. I then fanned the fern, mossy branches, acorns, and oak leaves out from these items on both sides of the piece, as shown in the photograph on page 88. You can work with whatever materials you have on hand to complete the look of your Woodland Garden.

 Honeysuckle Rose

*An abundance of invasive wild vines can be a good thing if the vines
are used creatively. When I pulled this wild honeysuckle from our trees,
it seemed a shame to waste it. Although stripping honeysuckle is
labor-intensive, the end result is a look you'll get with nothing else. As
you admire the finished wreath, you'll agree it is well worth the trouble.*

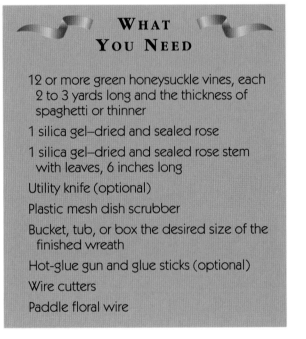

WHAT YOU NEED

12 or more green honeysuckle vines, each
  2 to 3 yards long and the thickness of
  spaghetti or thinner

1 silica gel–dried and sealed rose

1 silica gel–dried and sealed rose stem
  with leaves, 6 inches long

Utility knife (optional)

Plastic mesh dish scrubber

Bucket, tub, or box the desired size of the
  finished wreath

Hot-glue gun and glue sticks (optional)

Wire cutters

Paddle floral wire

WHAT YOU DO

1. Peel the exterior skin from the vine. If the
honeysuckle is green and young, its skin will be
tender; simply run your thumbnail down one side
of the vine, making a small slit in the outer brown
skin. If the vine is older, or if you want to save

your nails, use the utility knife to slit the skin.
Once it's been slit, the outer skin will peel away
from around the vine. I peel only a few feet at a
time because the vine will dry out quickly once
the skin has been removed.

2. Remove the fine, greenish white membrane that remains on the honeysuckle vine. (I find that if this membrane is left on, the vine takes on a dirty white appearance. The wreath will look much cleaner and more attractive if the membrane is removed.) To remove the membrane, grasp the peeled vine with one hand, and hold the dish scrubber in the other hand. Firmly wrap the scrubber around the vine, and slide it up and down the section of the vine you have peeled. Working under running water will help this scrubbing effort. (I do this at the kitchen sink, letting the peelings drop into the sink for cleanup later.) The newly scrubbed vine will feel a little slimy until the surface dries.

3. Repeat Steps 1 and 2 until the vine is thoroughly stripped. Coil this vine inside the bucket or box in which you'll form the wreath. (See "Making a Wreath Form" on page 46.) The vine doesn't have to lie flat; curves and irregularities add interest to the finished wreath.

4. Continue stripping each individual length of vine, coiling each piece in the bucket or box as it is stripped, and tucking the end of each newly added piece into the previously coiled vine.

5. Leave the wreath in the bucket or box for one to two weeks or until it is completely dry. Carefully remove it from the box. Because the vines dried in a circular shape, that is the shape they will retain, and the wreath will hold together quite well if handled carefully. I occasionally put small amounts of hot glue in places where the vines overlap to give the wreath added rigidity. Snip off any wild ends that stick out past the outside edges of the wreath. Using the wire, form a hanger and attach it to the back of the wreath.

6. Hot-glue the rose to the rose stem with leaves, and hot-glue the rose in place across the base of the wreath, as shown in the photograph on page 91.

GREAT NEST MATERIAL

One Christmas, I decorated the tree with tinsel, along with other trimmings. When the holidays were over and the ornaments were removed, some tinsel stayed on the tree when it was put outside. I later discovered that the birds gathered bits of the tinsel and used it in their nests. Once abandoned, the brightly decorated nests made fun accents to use in my wreaths. Now I occasionally make a conscious effort to put out other interesting things for the birds to use in nests, such as the stripped skin from honeysuckle vines. Occasionally, the birds will use my offerings to make a nest that I can actually retrieve and use in other projects. Sometimes I never see the material again, and that's okay, too. I know the birds put it to good use.

Season's Greetings

The nice thing about using preserved greenery in a holiday piece is that it does not dry out and shatter like fresh greenery does, so the piece can be put away to be used again the following year. And even though it isn't fresh, the greenery retains its wonderful evergreen fragrance.

WHAT YOU NEED

2 birch branches with catkins, each 20 inches long

2 flat boughs of preserved greenery, each 20 inches long (I used preserved cedar and black spruce)

2 stems of air-dried burgundy amaranthus, one 18 inches long and one 20 inches long

3 pinecones, each 5 inches long

1 dried honey locust pod

8 to 10 stems of air-dried rose hips

3 large dried pomegranates

Sticks or sturdy twigs to use as stems for the pinecones, locust pod, rose hips, and pomegranates

6 to 8 stems of short oak branches with the acorns attached

1 dried orange slice

2½ yards of wire-edged burgundy ribbon, 1¾ inches wide

Wire cutters

Paddle floral wire

Hot-glue gun and glue sticks

Scissors or shears

Gold spray paint

White craft paint and a small paintbrush

Paper plate

Transparent tape

WHAT YOU DO

1. Use the wire cutters to snip off several short pieces of birch from the branches, and set them aside to use later at the top of the swag. Make a base for the swag by wiring and gluing the birch branches together, as shown in the diagram. Wrap the paddle floral wire around the base, and make a wire loop hanger.

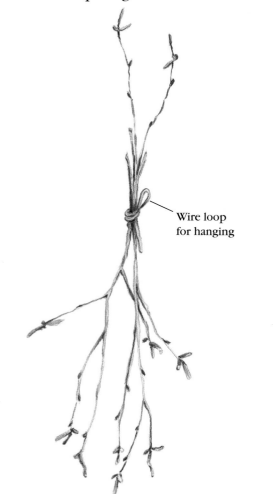

Wire loop for hanging

WIRING THE BRANCHES TOGETHER

2. Clip three 6-inch pieces of the preserved greenery from the bottom of the main boughs, and set them aside. Hot-glue the ends of the remaining boughs to the working center of the arrangement, making sure they extend down over

the birch branches. Glue the two stems of burgundy amaranthus to the working center of the swag (see "What Is the 'Working Center'?" on page 47), positioning them so that the amaranthus extends down over the greenery.

3. Create stems for the three pinecones using the sticks or twigs. (See "Creating Stems for Heavy Materials" on page 40.) Cut one stem 4 inches long, one 7 inches long, and one 10 inches long, and generously hot-glue a stem to the base of each pinecone. Hot-glue the ends of the stems to the working center of the arrangement so that the pinecones extend down over the greenery. Add a stem to the locust pod, and then glue the stem to the working center of the swag so that the pod falls down between the lower two pinecones.

4. Pour a little white craft paint onto the paper plate. Dip the paintbrush into the paint, and lightly brush the tips of the pinecones. This does not have to be exact; you can brush the top surfaces sometimes, and other times brush the undersides. Do this carefully to avoid getting paint on the other materials in the swag. Let the paint dry before proceeding.

5. Hot-glue a few of the stems of rose hips together to form a cluster, and add a stick stem. Glue the end of the stem of rose hips to the working center of the arrangement so that the rose hips fall between the lower two pinecones, as shown in the photograph on page 93.

6. Make the ribbon loops and tails for the swag. Cut two pieces of ribbon 8 inches long to make two 4-inch loops; two pieces 10 inches long for two 5-inch loops; and one piece 12 inches long for one 6-inch loop. Make the loops, and secure the ends of the ribbon with the transparent tape, as shown in "Making Ribbon Loops and Tails" on page 56. Cut the remaining piece of ribbon into two tails, one 8 inches long and one 25 inches long. Cut one end of each ribbon tail at an angle, and gather the other end of each tail, and secure it with transparent tape.

7. Hot-glue the ribbon loops and tails in place, as shown in the photograph on page 93.

8. Create stems for the pomegranates, using the sticks or sturdy twigs. Hot-glue the pomegranates to the working center, as shown in the photograph on page 93.

9. Hot-glue a single stem of rose hips behind the top pomegranate, pointing upward. Create another cluster of rose hips from the remaining stems by gluing their ends together. Glue this cluster to the working center, behind and between the lower two pomegranates.

10. Set aside a few stems of the oak branches to add to the top of the arrangement. Spray the remaining stems of the oak branches with gold spray paint, and allow them to dry. When completely dry, glue the stems into the swag, as shown in the photograph on page 93.

11. Hot-glue the orange slice to the base of the arrangement, placing it behind and below the top pomegranate. Glue the reserved pieces of birch branches, greenery, and oak branches onto the top of the swag for height.

EVERLASTING EVERGREENS

One thing to keep in mind when drying foliage of any kind in silica gel is that when dry, it is very crisp and needs to be handled carefully. The little petiole that holds a leaf or needle to a fresh branch is tiny to begin with and is reduced in size even more when the branch is dried. Even an accidental bump of your hand can disturb that little connection and knock off a leaf or many needles. Leaves can be reglued easily enough, but trying to reglue needles that have come off would be quite a chore. For this reason, when I'm incorporating evergreen foliage into a piece, I use varieties that have been commercially preserved. They are soft and flexible, are easily handled and don't shatter, and they retain their color for years.

If you wish to work with evergreen foliage from your yard, try placing the foliage in arrangements or wall pieces in its fresh state and letting it dry in place. (I wouldn't recommend this for door pieces that will be subject to the motion of a door opening and closing.) The boughs may remain intact for quite a while, but over time they will lose their green coloring and take on a whole new and interesting look. If you have room, consider storing pieces you have made until the following fall season. Think how pretty a dried centerpiece woud be with the beautiful bronze, tan, and rust tones of materials like dried evergreens, pinecones, magnolia leaves, and nandina berries.

Found Objects

ITEMS THAT YOU WOULDN'T ordinarily consider using as containers for dried floral arrangements can sometimes produce surprisingly wonderful results. Almost anything you may find tucked away in the attic—from old boxes to rusty pans to odd-shaped baskets—can serve as the base for an arrangement. The next time you run across some unusual treasure, take on the challenge!

97

$\mathcal{S}$pring from a Drawer

*Several years ago, I picked up a pair of drawers that had come from
an old treadle sewing machine, thinking they'd be pretty on my windowsill
with colorful plants in them. They were lovely, but then I had to see
what one would look like as a container for dried flowers.
The end result was a colorful piece I could enjoy all year long.*

3 silica gel–dried and sealed daffodils with stems, one 5, one 6, and one 9 inches long

2 silica gel–dried and sealed stems of flowering quince, one 11 and one 13 inches long

1 silica gel–dried and sealed stem of purple lilac with leaves, 10 inches tall

2 silica gel–dried and sealed stargazer lilies, each with a stem 12 inches long

1 silica gel–dried and sealed stem for stargazer lilies, 12 inches long

5 silica gel–dried and sealed pink peony tulips, each with a stem 4 to 8 inches long

6 silica gel–dried and sealed pansies (I used 3 deep blue and 3 purple and white), each with a stem 4 to 5 inches long

6 silica gel–dried and sealed pink bachelor's-buttons, each with a stem 3 to 4 inches long

7 to 9 stems of air-dried dark purple statice, each 6 to 10 inches long

2 stems of air-dried lavender statice, each 3 to 4 inches long

5 stems of preserved ivy, each 4 to 6 inches long

6 to 8 silica gel–dried and sealed tansy leaves, each 4 to 8 inches long

3 silica gel–dried and sealed tulip leaves, each 6 to 8 inches long

10 silica gel–dried and sealed pachysandra leaves

Square or rectangular container

Green Spanish moss

Serrated knife

Floral foam

Wire cutters

Hot-glue gun and glue sticks

Green spray paint for stems and leaves (optional)

WHAT YOU DO

1. Using the serrated knife, cut the floral foam to fit into the sewing machine drawer so that it extends about 1 inch above the top edge of the drawer. If it does not fit snugly in the drawer, secure it in place either by wedging it in with smaller pieces of foam or by hot gluing it (see "Designing Arrangements" on page 52). Cover the foam with the Spanish moss.

2. If desired, spray the leaves and stem material with the green spray paint, as described in "Spray Painting Leaves" on page 40. Set them aside to dry.

3. Make stems for the daffodils as described in "Daffodils" on page 27, and make stems for the other silica gel–dried flowers as described in "Adding a Stem" on page 38, referring to the materials list for stem lengths. Reconstruct the pistils and stamen of the lilies if you wish, as described in "Lilies" on page 26. Stand the flowers upright in a sturdy glass until you are ready to place them in the arrangement.

4. Using the photograph on the opposite page as a guide for placement, begin placing the flowers into the floral foam. The quince, lilac, and stem of lilies are placed in the back. Stems of blue statice are placed in line with these flowers, but below the lilies and quince, as shown. All other flowers are placed in front.

5. When all of the flowers are in place, insert the ivy into the floral foam below the pansies and the bachelor's-buttons at the front of the arrangement. Add the tansy and tulip leaves for contrast between the flowers or to fill in the gaps.

Simple Gifts

When we were little girls, my cousin gave this fishing basket to my sister and me to use as a handbag. I have kept it with me through the years, filling it with fresh flowers, putting it away for a while, and then getting it out again. By filling it with dried flowers, I've dressed it up and can display it year-round.

14 to 16 silica gel–dried and sealed zinnias in assorted sizes and colors

6 to 8 silica gel–dried and sealed stems of Blue Elf delphinium, each 4 to 8 inches long

5 to 7 air- or silica gel–dried and sealed stems of blue salvia, each 4 to 8 inches long

3 stems of silica gel–dried and sealed Panicle hydrangea (*Hydrangea paniculata*) with leaves, each 5 to 8 inches long

3 silica gel–dried and sealed Queen-Anne's-lace blossoms, each with a stem 6 to 8 inches long

Stem material for the silica gel–dried flowers

4 to 6 stems of air-dried wild grasses, each 8 to 13 inches long

8 to 10 stems of air- or silica gel–dried and sealed goldenrod, each 6 to 14 inches long

Small fishing or other basket (mine is approximately 8 x 4 x 6 inches)

Serrated knife

Floral foam

Small rocks

Green Spanish moss

Wire cutters

Sturdy drinking glass

Hot-glue gun and glue sticks

WHAT YOU DO

1. Use the serrated knife to cut the floral foam so that it fits inside the basket snugly and extends about 1 inch above the top edge of the basket. If you use a fishing basket, the base of the basket will be wider than the top, so cut the foam so that it has a gap of ¾ to 1 inch at the sides.

2. Secure the floral foam in place either by wedging it in with smaller pieces of foam or by gluing it to the basket. For added weight, place a few small rocks between the floral foam and the sides of the basket. Cover the foam with the Spanish moss.

3. Create stems for the silica gel–dried flowers, referring to "Adding a Stem" on page 38 and to the materials list for stem lengths. Stand the flowers upright in the sturdy drinking glass until you are ready to place the flowers in the arrangement.

4. Working from the center back of the basket, insert a 13-inch-long stem of wild grass into the floral foam. Place a 14-inch stem of goldenrod to the left of the grass and a 12-inch stem of goldenrod between them. Using these stem lengths to get you started, continue working from the back to the front of the arrangement and from the top down. Take time to create a nice mix of flowers, keeping in mind the juxtaposed colors, shapes, and densities of the flowers as you work.

Boxed Gatherings

*My grandmother kept this cigar box for many years. We were delighted
to discover it held a surprise—little crocheted baskets featured in
"Garden Party" on page 85. The wonderful earth tones of the cigar box
inspired this arrangement.*

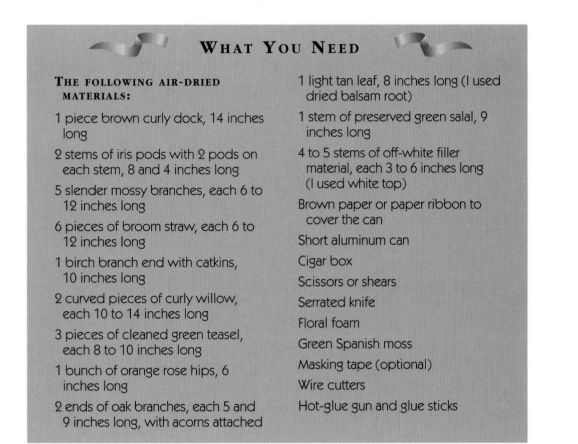

WHAT YOU NEED

THE FOLLOWING AIR-DRIED MATERIALS:

1 piece brown curly dock, 14 inches long

2 stems of iris pods with 2 pods on each stem, 8 and 4 inches long

5 slender mossy branches, each 6 to 12 inches long

6 pieces of broom straw, each 6 to 12 inches long

1 birch branch end with catkins, 10 inches long

2 curved pieces of curly willow, each 10 to 14 inches long

3 pieces of cleaned green teasel, each 8 to 10 inches long

1 bunch of orange rose hips, 6 inches long

2 ends of oak branches, each 5 and 9 inches long, with acorns attached

1 light tan leaf, 8 inches long (I used dried balsam root)

1 stem of preserved green salal, 9 inches long

4 to 5 stems of off-white filler material, each 3 to 6 inches long (I used white top)

Brown paper or paper ribbon to cover the can

Short aluminum can

Cigar box

Scissors or shears

Serrated knife

Floral foam

Green Spanish moss

Masking tape (optional)

Wire cutters

Hot-glue gun and glue sticks

WHAT YOU DO

1. Using the scissors, cut a piece of brown paper or paper ribbon to cover the outside of the aluminum can. Hot-glue the paper to the can. Using the serrated knife, cut a piece of floral foam that fits inside the can and extends up past the top edge about ¾ inch. Cover the foam with the green Spanish moss. Place the can inside the box. If you wish, secure it to the bottom of the box by sticking a piece of looped masking tape to the bottom of the can before you place it in the box.

CLEANING TEASEL

Teasel looks best when its head is free of spent blossoms and other things that may get caught up in its teeth. Often, teasel gathered from the wild will need some attention before it's used in an arrangement. Because the teasel stems are quite prickly, I find it best to wear leather gloves while handling them. This may be hard to believe, but the quickest way to clean a teasel head is with another teasel head! Grasp the stem of a teasel right below its head. Holding one in each hand, brush one head over the other, rotating each as you go. Both come out wonderfully clean.

2. Using the clippers, cut an 11-inch piece from the curly dock, and insert it in the center back of the floral foam inside the can, hot-gluing it in place. Using the photograph on page 102 as a guide for placement, hot-glue the 8-inch stem of iris pods to the left of the curly dock, and a 12-inch mossy branch to the left of the iris pods.

3. Place an 8-inch piece of the broom straw to the right of the curly dock, and place the birch branch to the right of the broom straw, hot-gluing them in place. In front of this grouping, in the center, hot-glue a curved piece of curly willow in the floral foam so that it comes up out of the foam about 3 inches and curves down to the left. Hot-glue another piece of upward-curved curly willow to the left of this grouping.

4. Working from the back to the front of the arrangement, continue hot-gluing the cleaned teasel (see "Cleaning Teasel" above), broom straw, rose hips, mossy branches, oak branches, iris pods, and light tan leaf into the floral foam, using the photograph on page 102 as a guide for placement.

5. Fill in between these materials with the preserved salal, the shorter pieces of curly dock, and the off-white filler material, using hot glue to secure them in place.

Momo's Basket

Although their blossoms are very fragile when dried, sweet peas have such a unique shape and look to them that it's worth the effort to dry them. In this arrangement, I've wrapped a pea vine around the wicker circle that holds this little copper planter, which came from my grandmother's— Momo's—attic.

WHAT YOU NEED

24 to 35 silica gel–dried and sealed sweet peas, each with a stem 4 to 8 inches long

1 to 3 silica gel–dried and sealed sweet pea vines

Container or planter (my planter is 3 inches high and 3 inches across)

Toothpicks and other stem materials

Serrated knife

Floral foam

30-gauge wrapped beading wire

Wire cutters

WHAT YOU DO

1. Using the serrated knife, carefully cut a piece of floral foam to snugly fit into the planter and extend up over the rim by approximately ½ inch. Slide the foam into the planter. Set aside some lengths of vine with leaves. Wrap the dried pea vine around the circle holding the planter, and then secure it in place with the beading wire.

2. Create stems for the sweet peas, referring to "Adding a Stem" on page 38, and referring to the materials list for stem lengths.

3. Insert the stems of the sweet peas into the foam. Vary the stem lengths, and add an occasional length of vine with leaves for contrast. Bring some leaves down over the planter's edges.

Springtime Masterpiece

Although working with glass containers or vases presents some challenges, don't rule out working with a favorite or interesting glass piece. To create a pretty arrangement, try using different kinds of glass, including tinted, etched, or even crackled glass.

WHAT YOU NEED

THE FOLLOWING SILICA GEL—DRIED AND SEALED MATERIALS:

2 pink Asiatic lilies with stems 12 and 14 inches long

6 stems purple lilac with leaves, each with a stem 12 to 15 inches long

2 pink peonies, each with a stem 12 inches long

1 stargazer lily with a stem 12 inches long

2 monarda of any color, each with a stem 17 inches long

2 stems of blue delphinium, one 13 and one 20 inches long

4 stems of purple larkspur, each 16 to 18 inches long

8 Shasta daisies, each with a stem 10 to 14 inches long

3 pink gerbera daisies with stems 7, 8, and 9 inches long

2 stems of pink astilbe (can be air-dried, as well), one 18 and one 20 inches long

3 or 4 stems of quince foliage with stems, each 10 to 14 inches long

Stem material for flowers

8-inch blue wide-mouthed jar

Floral adhesive tape

Wire cutters

Scissors or shears

Hot-glue gun and glue sticks

WHAT YOU DO

1. Cut strips of the floral adhesive tape that are long enough to fit over the mouth of the jar and extend down the sides approximately ¾ inch. You can also cut the pieces of tape in half lengthwise so they aren't so wide. Place the pieces of tape over the mouth of the jar, taping the ends to the sides and creating a grid, as shown in the diagram.

Tape grid

CREATING A TAPED GRID

2. Using the materials list as a guide for stem lengths, create stems for the flowers as described in "Adding a Stem" on page 38. Stand the flowers upright in a sturdy glass until you are ready to place them in the arrangement.

3. Working from the center of the grid to the outside, arrange the materials in the jar, using the photograph on the opposite page as a guide for placement. The stems will rest up against the pieces of tape and can be hot-glued to the edges of the tape to keep them in position. When flower stems rest against the mouth of the jar, they can be glued in place there, as well.

4. This piece will have a free-form look and feel to it, as if it were just gathered from the garden. By creating groupings (placing several flowers of one variety together, as opposed to spacing them out throughout the piece), you will help create that look.

Fall for Fun

I found this pumpkin at a gift shop several years ago—it was originally designed to house a lit candle. Since I enjoy leaving it out during the entire fall season, I made a whimsical bittersweet headdress for it. I find one of the prettiest things about a bittersweet vine growing in the wild are all of the twists and curves to the vine as well as its interestingly shaped green leaves.

6 or 7 stems of air-dried bittersweet, each 10 to 15 inches long, with berries (see "Picking Bittersweet" on the opposite page for drying instructions)

7 to 10 pieces of silica gel–dried and sealed bittersweet vine, each 10 to 20 inches long, with leaves

5 to 8 stems of air-dried Japanese lanterns, each 8 to 15 inches long

Terra-cotta pumpkin (the pumpkin in the photograph is about 5 inches tall and 6½ inches wide)

Clay pot to fit inside the pumpkin (I used one 3 inches high and 3 inches across)

Serrated knife

Floral foam

Green Spanish moss

Wire cutters

Hot-glue gun and glue sticks

WHAT YOU DO

1. Dry the bittersweet vine with the leaves in silica gel (refer to the Flower Drying Timetable on page 159). If you have difficulty finding a container long enough to dry the bittersweet vine with the leaves attached, wrap up the vine into a circle, or bend it to fit into a container, as described in "Making a Wreath Form" on page 46. Don't dry the parts of the vine with berries in silica gel, or all of the yellow petals will fall off (see "Picking Bittersweet").

2. When the vine is dry and you are ready to assemble the arrangement, use the serrated knife to cut the floral foam to fit inside the small clay pot, cutting the top of the foam even with the rim of the pot. Cover the foam with the Spanish moss. Choose a few nicely curved pieces of the bittersweet vine with leaves, and insert them into the top of the floral foam, toward the back. (The pumpkin shown in the photograph on the oppo-site page contains a one-sided arrangement. To make a two-sided arrangement, begin in the center of the floral foam, and you will need additional bittersweet and Japanese lanterns.) Add some sprigs of bittersweet with berries and stems of Japanese lanterns, using the photograph on the opposite page as a guide for placement. Bring the materials down the sides and around the front until the arrangement is complete.

3. This arrangement is supposed to have a loose look, and to achieve that, you may need to trim some lanterns off the individual branches, or the arrangement may take on a more dense, packed look. You'll want the curves of the vine and berry branches to show, and if too much material is added, that look will be lost. Fill in the bottom of the arrangement with individual leaves from the bittersweet by gluing them to stems of the other materials.

Gladys Goose

Gladys was a real find at a local craft show. I know she's really a duck, but this name just seems to follow her around. I use her to hold lots of things, from small pots of pansies or primroses in the spring to small dried arrangements in the fall and winter. In the summer, she often holds dried flowers from my cutting garden, as she is doing here.

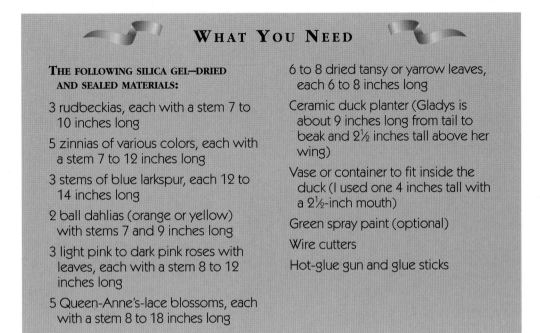

THE FOLLOWING SILICA GEL—DRIED AND SEALED MATERIALS:

3 rudbeckias, each with a stem 7 to 10 inches long

5 zinnias of various colors, each with a stem 7 to 12 inches long

3 stems of blue larkspur, each 12 to 14 inches long

2 ball dahlias (orange or yellow) with stems 7 and 9 inches long

3 light pink to dark pink roses with leaves, each with a stem 8 to 12 inches long

5 Queen-Anne's-lace blossoms, each with a stem 8 to 18 inches long

6 to 8 dried tansy or yarrow leaves, each 6 to 8 inches long

Ceramic duck planter (Gladys is about 9 inches long from tail to beak and 2½ inches tall above her wing)

Vase or container to fit inside the duck (I used one 4 inches tall with a 2½-inch mouth)

Green spray paint (optional)

Wire cutters

Hot-glue gun and glue sticks

WHAT YOU DO

1. Spray the stem material and leaves with green spray paint if desired, as described in "Spray Painting Leaves" on page 40, and set them aside to dry. Create stems for the materials, referring to "Adding a Stem" on page 38 and to the materials list for stem lengths. For arrangements like this, I usually make the stems longer than I think I'll need so I don't end up with a stem that is too short. Stand the flowers upright in a sturdy glass until you are ready to place them in the arrangement.

2. Insert the vase or small container inside the duck planter.

3. Insert three or four stemmed flowers into the vase. They will rest against the rim of the vase because there is nothing to hold them in the bottom. Secure them in place at the rim of the vase with a drop of hot glue. Arrange this piece in the same way you'd arrange it if the flowers were fresh. Since I was trying to create a just-gathered-from-the-garden look, I assembled small groupings of flowers in the way do when I'm cutting fresh flowers from the garden, allowing some to overlap others or letting a few flowers stick out all by themselves.

4. Continue to add flowers into the vase. If you do create groupings, try to not let the flowers actually touch each other, because they are inflexible. To prevent the stems from wiggling around inside the vase, which can cause petals to break off, hot-glue the stems together where they cross each other. You may need to steam the stems of flowers to bend them so they'll fit into the lower part of the arrangement, as I did here. Add the foliage last, hot-gluing it to the stems, to give the piece a fuller, more natural look.

Container Concepts

OFTEN IT IS A CONTAINER OR VASE that serves as the inspiration for a dried flower arrangement. The color, shape, and texture of the container all play a role in your selection of flowers and natural materials. This chapter shows you some combinations that I think work particularly well together.

$\mathscr{A}$ Passion for Peonies

Heavy earthenware vases are handsome when displayed with arrangements that have a visual mass and weight to them as well. Peonies, which come in a variety of colors, sizes, and even shapes, make lovely mass arrangements. When accented with just a little foliage for splashes of contrast, they can easily hold the floor all by themselves.

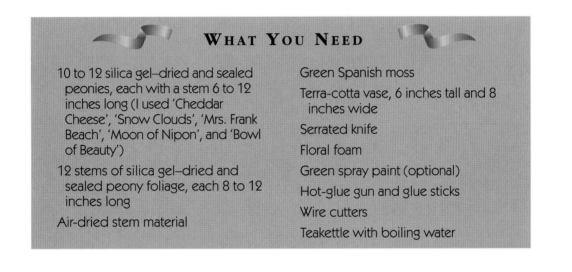

WHAT YOU NEED

10 to 12 silica gel–dried and sealed peonies, each with a stem 6 to 12 inches long (I used 'Cheddar Cheese', 'Snow Clouds', 'Mrs. Frank Beach', 'Moon of Nipon', and 'Bowl of Beauty')

12 stems of silica gel–dried and sealed peony foliage, each 8 to 12 inches long

Air-dried stem material

Green Spanish moss

Terra-cotta vase, 6 inches tall and 8 inches wide

Serrated knife

Floral foam

Green spray paint (optional)

Hot-glue gun and glue sticks

Wire cutters

Teakettle with boiling water

WHAT YOU DO

1. Use the serrated knife to cut the floral foam to fit the vase or container, extending it about ¾ inch above the rim of the vase. Cover the foam with the Spanish moss. If desired, spray the stem material and peony leaves with the green spray paint.

2. Hot-glue a 12-inch stem to the bottom of one peony so that the peony blossom is facing upward, and place the stem end in the center of the floral foam inside the vase. Working from the top down, add peony foliage to the arrangement, using the photograph on the opposite page as a guide for placement. Below the peony foliage, add peonies with stem lengths approximately 8 to 9 inches for the middle layer and 6 inches for the bottom layer. Alternate colors and types of peonies if you can as you work your way down and around the arrangement.

3. Work leaves in between the peonies, steaming them over the teakettle filled with boiling water if needed, to create curves that fit in and around the peonies easily. (See "Bending with Steam" on page 50.)

✦Spring Collection

*For displaying flowers, a wall pocket is a nice alternative to
the more traditional wreath or spray. I like the woven birch look
of this pocket because its light coloring doesn't visually overpower
the arrangement of brightly colored flowers.*

WHAT YOU DO

1. Use the serrated knife to carefully cut a
piece of floral foam that fits snugly inside the wall
pocket and extends approximately 1 inch above
the center of the rim. Use hot glue and position
the foam in place, then cover it with the green
Spanish moss.

2. Insert the preserved ivy into the floral
foam, as shown in the diagram on the opposite
page. Work with the unique curves of the ivy; it
doesn't have to be placed exactly as mine is. The
idea is to make the ivy look as if it's growing out
of the wall pocket.

2 sprigs of silica gel–dried and sealed purple larkspur, one 8 and one 9 inches long

10 stems of air-dried bicolor globe amaranth, each 4 to 10 inches long

2 stems of air-dried blue annual statice, each 6 inches long

1 silica gel–dried and sealed pink tulip with a stem 6 inches long

2 silica gel–dried and sealed yellow daffodils, each with a stem 4 to 5 inches long (see "Daffodils" on page 27)

4 silica gel–dried and sealed purple or lavender anemones, each with a stem 3 to 4 inches long

1 silica gel–dried and sealed pink zinnia with a stem 2 to 3 inches long

3 silica gel–dried and sealed purple and white pansies, each with a stem 2 to 3 inches long

3 silica gel–dried and sealed yellow primroses, each with a stem 2 to 3 inches long

7 to 9 pieces of preserved ivy, 4 to 10 inches long

Air-dried stem material

Single ivy leaves

A few stems of preserved plumosa fern, 5 to 6 inches long

Serrated knife

Floral foam

Green Spanish moss

10 x 4-inch wall pocket

Hot-glue gun and glue sticks

Wire cutters

Floral foam covered with green Spanish moss

Insert ivy

PLACING THE IVY IN FLORAL FOAM

3. Insert the larkspur and globe amaranth into the floral foam at the back of the wall pocket, as shown in the photograph on the opposite page. Place the annual statice to the right of the larkspur.

4. Create stems for the remaining silica gel–dried flowers, as described in "Adding a Stem" on page 38. Refer to the materials list for stem lengths. Stand the flowers upright in a sturdy glass until you are ready to place them in the arrangement.

5. Insert the flowers into the floral foam, using the photograph on the opposite page as a guide for placement. Then fill in between the individual flowers with the individual ivy leaves and plumosa ferns, covering the Spanish moss. Hot-glue the stems of the greenery to the stems of the flowers already in place.

Flower Girl

When thinking of creative ways to display dried flowers, consider bringing outdoor garden sculptures indoors. My sculptor friend Judy made this inviting piece with a wonderful apron pocket that can be filled with an assortment of flowers which can be changed seasonally.

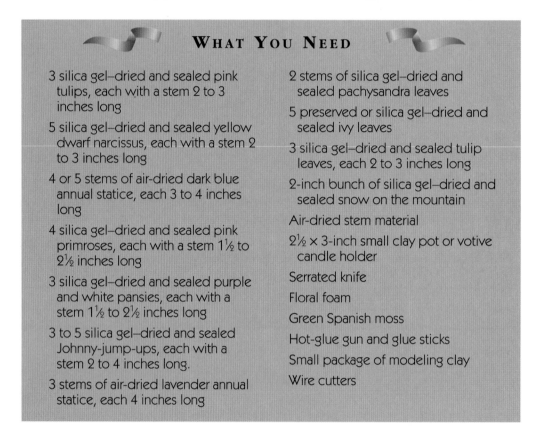

WHAT YOU NEED

- 3 silica gel–dried and sealed pink tulips, each with a stem 2 to 3 inches long
- 5 silica gel–dried and sealed yellow dwarf narcissus, each with a stem 2 to 3 inches long
- 4 or 5 stems of air-dried dark blue annual statice, each 3 to 4 inches long
- 4 silica gel–dried and sealed pink primroses, each with a stem 1½ to 2½ inches long
- 3 silica gel–dried and sealed purple and white pansies, each with a stem 1½ to 2½ inches long
- 3 to 5 silica gel–dried and sealed Johnny-jump-ups, each with a stem 2 to 4 inches long.
- 3 stems of air-dried lavender annual statice, each 4 inches long

- 2 stems of silica gel–dried and sealed pachysandra leaves
- 5 preserved or silica gel–dried and sealed ivy leaves
- 3 silica gel–dried and sealed tulip leaves, each 2 to 3 inches long
- 2-inch bunch of silica gel–dried and sealed snow on the mountain
- Air-dried stem material
- 2½ × 3-inch small clay pot or votive candle holder
- Serrated knife
- Floral foam
- Green Spanish moss
- Hot-glue gun and glue sticks
- Small package of modeling clay
- Wire cutters

WHAT YOU DO

1. Using the serrated knife, cut the floral foam so that it fits snugly inside the clay pot and extends about ¾ inch above the rim. Push the floral foam down into the clay pot, and cover it with a small amount of the Spanish moss. If necessary, use hot glue to hold the green Spanish moss in place.

2. Place the small clay pot in the apron pocket. Because the pocket is a slightly different shape than the pot, I used a small amount of modeling clay to hold the pot in the pocket at the angle I wanted and to keep the pot from rolling around inside the pocket. Press the clay around the parts of the pot that rest against the pocket.

3. Create stems for the silica gel–dried flowers, as described in "Adding a Stem" on page 38. Refer to the materials list for stem lengths. Stand the flowers upright in a small glass until you are ready to place them in the arrangement.

4. Starting at the back of the floral foam, insert the three pink tulips to the left of the center of the arrangement, using the photograph at left as a guide for placement. Use hot glue to secure them in place. Put the grouping of yellow dwarf narcissus to the right of the tulips, and insert the two pieces of dark blue annual statice on either side of the tulips and the narcissus.

5. Place a stem of pachysandra leaves in the center of the floral foam, and insert the stems of the primroses in the gaps between the leaves so that it looks as if they're growing out of the leaves.

6. Place a grouping of the purple and white pansies to the lower left of the tulips, and place a grouping of Johnny-jump-ups in the lower center of the apron pocket. Place a small grouping of lavender statice between the pansies and the Johnny-jump-ups.

7. Break apart the other stem of pachysandra leaves, and hot-glue those leaves, the ivy leaves, the tulip leaves, and the snow on the mountain into the spaces between the flower stems.

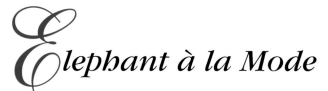

Elephant à la Mode

*When I was a child, my grandmother would seat my sister and me
at her dining room table and serve us tea and cookies. The sugar lumps
we added to our tea were special, but this elephant teapot was the real star
of the show. When I used him for this arrangement, I chose flowers that
picked up the bright colors of his saddle. Look at the teapot you'll be
using and choose flowers that complement its dominant colors.*

THE FOLLOWING SILICA GEL–DRIED AND SEALED MATERIALS:

3 stems of magenta coral bells, each 7 to 10 inches long

2 stems of bleeding hearts, each 8 inches long

4 stems dark blue delphinium, each 8 to 10 inches long

3 orange ball dahlias, each with a stem 5 to 8 inches long

1 purple dahlia with a stem 5 inches long

1 white anemone with a stem 6 inches long

2 stems of white snapdragons, one 8 and one 9 inches long

1 pale yellow columbine with a stem 8 inches long

1 pink-and-white daffodil with a stem 6 inches long

3 small peonies (3 to 4½ inches across), each with a stem 6 to 7 inches long (I used 'Karl Rosenfield' and 'La Cygne')

2 shasta daisies, each with a stem 6 inches long

1 lily-flowering tulip with a stem 7 inches long

1 small orange-and-yellow climbing rose with a stem 6 inches long

1 gloriosa lily with a stem 6 inches long

2 blue asters with stems 5 and 6 inches long

Columbine and peony foliage

Stem material

1 small square plastic container measuring 2½ inches across to fit inside the elephant, with the lid removed

Ceramic teapot

Serrated knife

Floral foam

Hot-glue gun and glue sticks

Green Spanish moss

Wire cutters

WHAT YOU DO

1. Using the knife, cut the floral foam so that it fits inside the small plastic container and extends ¾ inch above the top edge. Hot-glue the foam in place, and cover it with the Spanish moss. Place the plastic container inside the teapot.

2. Using the stem material, make stems for the flowers that need them, following the instructions in "Adding a Stem" on page 38. Use the materials list as a guide for stem length. Stand the flowers upright in a sturdy glass until you are ready to place them in the arrangement.

3. Beginning in the center of the floral foam, insert a 10-inch stem of delphinium and a 10-inch stem of coral bells. Using the photograph on the opposite page as a guide for placement, insert the other flower stems into the floral foam, working around and down the arrangement. As you work, think about juxtaposed colors and shapes of flowers so that longer spiky flowers are placed in between rounder, denser ones. Work greenery in between the flowers occasionally, and use it to fill in around the bottom as well. Don't hide any interesting features on the teapot.

Sensational Stargazers

The simple lines of glass vases share a regal quality with lilies. Often when I cut stems of fresh lilies from the garden, I do nothing more when arranging them as fresh flowers than stand them up in a glass vase. Here, I duplicated that look with a simple arrangement of stargazer lilies that can be enjoyed for months at a time.

What You Need

15 to 20 silica gel–dried and sealed stargazer lilies

5 to 7 air-dried lily stems

Silica gel–dried and sealed peony leaves, 10 to 12 per stem (if these are unavailable, substitute other leaves shaped like those of the lily)

Dried axis of pinnate leaves to replace the pistils and stamens of the lilies (see "Lilies" on page 26)

Glass vase 10 inches tall and 4 to 5 inches wide

Green and yellow spray paint

Wire cutters

Scissors or shears

Hot-glue gun and glue sticks

Teakettle with boiling water (optional)

What You Do

1. Follow the instructions for reconstructing lilies, as described in "Lilies" on page 26. Spray the lily stems and peony leaves with the green spray paint. Trim off individual leaflets from each grouping of peony leaves, as shown in the diagram. Attach the leaves to the dried lily stem with hot glue at the nodules that were left on the stems when their leaves were removed. If the leaves are too dry to work with easily, steam them over a teakettle filled with a small amount of boiling water to give them more flexibility.

2. Attach the lilies to the tips of the stems with hot glue. Carefully place each completed lily stem in the vase so that the flowers from one stem

don't rub up against those on another stem. If you wish, put a spot of hot glue on the outside of each stem where it rests against the vase's edge, to hold the stem in place.

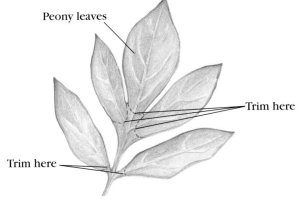

Peony leaves

Trim here

Trim here

TRIMMING OFF THE LEAFLETS

Grand Opening

Don't limit yourself to a small scale when working with dried flowers. There are so many larger, beautiful flowers that can be made into large, stunning arrangements such as this one.

THE FOLLOWING SILICA GEL—DRIED AND SEALED MATERIALS:

4 stems of delphinium (I used 3 stems of dark blue, 10 to 12 inches long, and a lighter lavender color, 23 inches long)

4 parrot tulips, each with a stem 18 inches long

1 apricot tulip, with a stem 18 inches long

1 Estelle Rijnveld (red and white) tulip, with a stem 12 inches long

2 Snow Parrot tulips, each with a stem 10 inches long

2 stems of stargazer lilies with 2 lilies on each stem, one 18 and one 8 inches long (prepared as described in "Lilies" on page 26)

4 stems of dark lavender-blue lilac with leaves, one each 16, 14, 12 and 6 inches long

3 large single red peonies, each with a stem 12 inches long (I used 'Lobata Red')

1 white peony with yellow center, with a stem 10 inches long (I used Moon of Nipon)

1 burgundy double peony, with a stem 8 inches long (I used Karl Rosenfield)

5 yellow roses, with stems 17, 16, 15, 8, and 6 inches long

10 stems of silica gel—dried and sealed quince and/or forsythia branches with leaves, each with stems 12 to 24 inches long

Air-dried stem materials

Plain ceramic container, 9 inches high with a mouth 4 inches across

Serrated knife

Floral foam

Green Spanish moss

Wire cutters

Hot-glue gun and glue sticks

WHAT YOU DO

1. Use the serrated knife to shave an inch off one side of the floral foam so that it measures 8 × 3 × 3 inches. Use sections of the piece you cut off to extend the floral foam 1 inch above the rim of the vase. (For instructions, see "Creating Arrangements in Tall Vases" on page 57.) Cover the foam with the Spanish moss.

2. Using the stem material, make stems for the flowers that need them, following the instructions in "Adding a Stem" on page 38. Use the materials list as a guide to stem length. Stand the flowers upright in a sturdy glass until you are ready to place them in the arrangement.

3. Working forward from the center back of the floral foam, place the 23-inch stem of delphinium next to an 18-inch branch of quince leaves, using the photograph on the opposite page as a guide for placement. To the lower left of the quince, place a 16-inch stem of lilac. To the lower right of the delphinium, add another 18-inch branch of quince, and below that, a 14-inch stem of lilac. The apricot and parrot tulips, the two yellow roses, and the stem of stargazer lilies are placed in front of these flowers.

4. Using the photograph on the opposite page as a guide, arrange the flowers working from the back to the front and the top down.

Garden Variety

*When choosing materials for this piece, I was interested in
bringing out the jar's subtle colors of rust and yellow and found them
in a variety of natural materials.*

12 to 14 stems of silica gel–dried and sealed goldenrod, each 6 to 14 inches long

6 silica gel–dried and sealed stems of quince foliage, each 6 to 12 inches long

3 air-dried stems of field grass, each 9 to 12 inches long

4 air-dried stems of nandina berries, each 6 to 10 inches long

7 silica gel–dried and sealed yellow calla lilies, each with a stem 4 to 9 inches long

4 silica gel–dried and sealed yellow Asiatic lilies, each with a stem 5 to 20 inches long

1 silica gel–dried and sealed gloriosa lily with a stem 5 inches long

2 silica gel–dried and sealed orange tiger lilies, each with a stem 6 inches long

6 silica gel–dried and sealed stems of forsythia foliage, each 8 to 12 inches long

6 air-dried stems of hydrangea, each 4 to 8 inches long

3 air-dried stems of curly dock, each 8 to 10 inches long

1 air-dried stem of privit berries, 11 inches long

Silica gel–dried and sealed stem material

Ceramic ginger jar, 7 inches tall

Serrated knife

Floral foam

Hot-glue gun and glue sticks

Green Spanish moss

Green 30-gauge floral wire

Wire cutters

WHAT YOU DO

1. Using the serrated knife, trim the block of floral foam so that it measures $8 \times 2\frac{1}{2} \times 2\frac{1}{2}$ inches and so that it will fit down inside the ginger jar snugly. Hot-glue the foam to the inside bottom of the jar, if desired. Cover the foam with the green Spanish moss.

2. Insert a 14-inch piece of goldenrod, a 12-inch piece of quince foliage, and a 12-inch piece of field grass into the center of the floral foam, angling out slightly, as shown in the photograph on the opposite page.

3. Using the stem material, make stems for the flowers that need, them following the instructions in "Adding a Stem" on page 38. Use the materials list as a guide to stem length. Stand the flowers upright in a sturdy glass until you are ready to place them in the arrangement.

4. Using the photograph on the opposite page as a guide for placement, insert the other materials and flowers into the arrangement, working around the piece from the top down. After the nandina berries are placed, cut a piece of floral wire as long as each cluster, and insert it into the foam next to the stem of each cluster. Hot-glue the wire to the stem of the berries in a couple of places to help support the weight of the cluster.

# A Touch of Glass

This romantic and classy arrangement was created by using white and off-white flowers in stemmed glassware. It makes an attractive centerpiece for a quiet candlelit dinner or for any other formal occasion.

WHAT YOU NEED

THE FOLLOWING SILICA GEL—DRIED AND SEALED MATERIALS:

5 small white calla lilies, each blossom 3 to 4 inches long

8 stems of quince branches with small leaves, each 4 to 6 inches long

3 white or off-white anemones, each with a stem 2 to 4 inches long

4 stems of white freesia, each 3 inches long (dry the stems and blossoms separately and reattach before using)

1 white ranunculus, with a stem 2 inches long

3 off-white or white roses, each with a stem 2 inches long

1 branch of dogwood with approximately 7 blossoms, 7 inches long

2 white Asian lilies, with stems 2 and 4 inches long

4 small clusters of green and white euphorbia leaves, each 4 to 6 inches long

6 stems of mature quince branches with larger leaves, each 6 to 9 inches long (cut in summer)

Air-dried stem material

Stemmed glass

Serrated knife

Floral foam

Hot-glue gun and glue sticks

Green Spanish moss

Floral tape (optional)

Wire cutters

WHAT YOU DO

1. Use the knife to cut the floral foam so it fits into the bowl of the glass and extends 1 inch above the rim. Apply hot-glue to the bottom corners of the foam, and place it into the glass. (If you want to remove the foam, hot glue will pop off glassware easily with a little effort.) Cover the foam with Spanish moss. If desired, secure the foam by placing floral tape over the top of the foam and pressing the ends to the outside top edge of the glass.

2. Prepare the dogwood branch as shown in "Bending with Steam" on page 50; the lilies, as described in "Lilies" on page 26. Hot-glue a 1-inch stem to one calla lily, and make stems for the other flowers that need them, following the instructions in "Adding a Stem" on page 38. Use the materials list as a guide to stem length. Stand the flowers in a sturdy glass until you are ready to arrange them.

3. Insert the calla lily into the center of the floral foam. Add the quince branches near the center on either side of the calla lily, and add the anemone near the top center.

4. Working from the center out and down, add the remaining flowers and foliage to the piece, using the photograph on the opposite page as a guide for placement until you have a pleasing arrangement. As you look down at the top of the piece, it should be oval in shape. Allow the quince foliage to curve down over the sides of the glass.

Tradition, Tradition

WHILE SOME FLORAL DESIGNERS are drawn to experiment with unusual ways to present their dried materials, others appreciate a more traditional approach. Choosing the right materials and arranging them with flair is the key to creating eye-catching and exciting traditional designs.

Backyard Gatherings

Don't overlook the treasures that are simply lying on the ground in your own backyard or neighborhood. The magnolia leaves and pinecones used here were simply picked up off the ground.

WHAT YOU NEED

20-inch-diameter grapevine wreath

10 to 12 air-dried salal leaves, each 3 to 4 inches long

Assortment of pinecones of varying lengths and widths (I used 7 Norway spruce cones, each 5 inches long; 3 white-pine cones, each 2½ inches long; 3 blue spruce cones, each 3 inches long; 2 cedar cones, each 2 inches long; and 3 Scotch pine cones, each 3 inches long)

5 blue spruce cones

4 red spruce cones

3 large air-dried pomegranates

4 silica gel–dried and sealed white roses of varied sizes

Stem material for the roses

Assortment of small, medium, and large air-dried magnolia leaves

5 cotton bolls

5 to 10 sprigs of other greenery or leaves for filler, each 3 to 5 inches long (I used preserved cedar and poplar)

Grapevine tendrils

10 sprigs of flat blue-green eucalyptus, each 4 to 6 inches long

2¼ yards of wire-edged gold mesh ribbon, 2½ inches wide

30-gauge wrapped beading wire

Wire cutters

Gold spray paint

Hot-glue gun and glue sticks

Transparent tape

Scissors or shears

Ruler or yardstick

WHAT YOU DO

1. Cut the wire or cord on the grapevine wreath, and rework the material, as shown in "How to Reduce the Density of a Grapevine Wreath" on page 47. By removing some of the vine and creating a new, looser shape, the wreath will be a more suitable base for the other materials. Secure the new wreath with the wire in several places.

2. Paint the salal leaves using the gold spray paint, as described in "Spray Painting Leaves" on page 40, and set them aside to dry.

3. Working with the natural hills and valleys of the grapevine wreath base, make stems for the Norway spruce and white-pine cones, as described in "Creating Stems for Heavy Materials" on page 40.

Using the photograph on page 132 as a guide for placement, nestle the pinecones into the base so that they are glued down into the wreath and are not just resting on top of it. I pointed most of the cones in the same direction but turned a few in the opposite direction to create visual interest. Notice that some are grouped together and others are placed by themselves for variety.

4. Add the pomegranates and Scotch pine cones to the grapevine form so that they move the eye around the wreath. Add stems to the four roses, following the instructions in "Adding a Stem" on page 38, and hot-glue them in place, as shown in the photograph on page 132.

5. Hot-glue the magnolia leaves in behind the pinecones and roses to fill in the background and add width to the piece. Again, I pointed most of the leaves in one general direction, but I varied this in several places to add visual interest. For example, at the lower right side, where several items are clustered together, I grouped different-size leaves and glued them so they radiated out from behind the cluster.

6. Hot-glue the cotton bolls, gold salal leaves, and remaining pinecones where they are needed to create visual balance and density. Because the cotton bolls, gold leaves, and roses are light in color and contrast nicely against the brown color of the other materials, place them so that they draw the eye around the wreath.

7. Cut five 10-inch pieces of ribbon, and make each one into a 5-inch loop, securing the ends with transparent tape. (See "Making Ribbon Loops and Tails" on page 56.) Cut the remaining length of ribbon into three tails, one 7 inches long and two 10 inches long. Gather and tape one end of each tail, and cut the other end of each tail at an angle.

8. Glue the ribbons in place behind the roses, as shown in the photograph on page 132. If there are places in the wreath where the mechanics need to be concealed or the wreath isn't visually balanced or rounded, use sprigs of greenery, eucalyptus, or any remaining magnolia leaves to fill in. Give the finished wreath some extra interest by hot-gluing extra grapevine tendrils to the front and sides.

Sunday's Child

This small silver cup filled with small, delicate flowers is a beautiful gift to celebrate the birth of a child. It brings to mind the familiar poem that begins, "Monday's child is fair of face...."

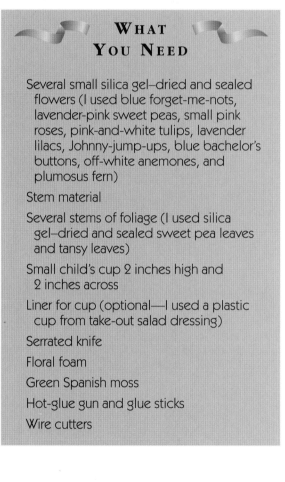

WHAT YOU NEED

Several small silica gel–dried and sealed flowers (I used blue forget-me-nots, lavender-pink sweet peas, small pink roses, pink-and-white tulips, lavender lilacs, Johnny-jump-ups, blue bachelor's buttons, off-white anemones, and plumosus fern)

Stem material

Several stems of foliage (I used silica gel–dried and sealed sweet pea leaves and tansy leaves)

Small child's cup 2 inches high and 2 inches across

Liner for cup (optional—I used a plastic cup from take-out salad dressing)

Serrated knife

Floral foam

Green Spanish moss

Hot-glue gun and glue sticks

Wire cutters

WHAT YOU DO

1. Use the serrated knife to cut a piece of floral foam to fit snugly inside the cup (or liner, if you choose to use one). Cover the foam with the Spanish moss.

2. Use hot glue to add stems to the dried flowers as needed to make them approximately ½ to 1½ times the height of the cup. For this cup, I made the stems 1 to 3 inches long. (See "Adding a Stem" on page 38.)

3. Working from the center out, carefully insert the stems of the flowers and foliage into the floral foam, using the photograph above as a guide.

$\mathcal{T}$raditional Twig Wreath

An elegant way to dress up a twig wreath is simply to mix flowers that have different blooming times.

WHAT YOU NEED

16-inch-diameter twig wreath

16 to 20 sprigs of preserved green boxwood, each 3 to 6 inches long

24 air-dried or preserved acutely pointed single leaves (like those of laurel or camellia) in varying green colors, 2 to 3 inches long

3 silica gel–dried and sealed roses of different colors

1 silica gel–dried and sealed burgundy zinnia

6 to 7 stems of air-dried blue annual statice, each 3 to 5 inches long

3 clusters of silica gel–dried and sealed purple lilac, each 3 to 4 inches long

6 to 8 small clusters of silica gel–dried and sealed hydrangea

12 to 14 stems of silica gel–dried and sealed goldenrod, each 4 to 5 inches long

Toothpicks

Hot-glue gun and glue sticks

Wire cutters

WHAT YOU DO

1. If the twig wreath base is dense, remove some of the twigs. Hot-glue most of the boxwood and some of the single leaves in place, as shown in the diagram.

2. Use toothpicks to make short stems for the silica gel–dried flowers, following the instructions in "Adding a Stem" on page 38. Hot-glue the roses and zinnias to the wreath, referring to the photograph on the opposite page. Clip off any parts of stems that extend past the back of the wreath.

3. Fill in around the flowers with the statice, lilac, and hydrangea. Add the goldenrod and remaining pieces of boxwood and leaves to fill in the spaces.

PLACING BOXWOOD AND LEAVES ON BASE

Botanically Baroque

This piece, designed to have a baroque look, carries some nice visual weight. Many of the materials I used in it were large and dense, so I chose a heavy, wire-edged tapestry ribbon to complement them.

WHAT YOU NEED

20-inch-long grapevine arch

3 sprigs of flat air-dried eucalyptus, each 9 inches long

3 to 5 pinecones, each 1½ to 2½ inches long

2 white-pine cones, each 4 to 5 inches long

2 spruce cones, each 3 inches long

3 large air-dried pomegranates

3 medium air-dried artichokes

4 clusters of air-dried tetragonia pods, each 4 inches across

Stem material for the pinecones, pomegranates, artichokes, and tetragonia

2 clusters of green and burgundy hydrangea, each 2½ inches across

Sprigs of preserved greenery, such as juniper or cedar

Grapevine tendrils

1½ yards of burgundy tapestry ribbon, 2½ inches wide

30-gauge wrapped beading wire

Wire cutters

Scissors or shears

Transparent tape

Hot-glue gun and glue sticks

WHAT YOU DO

1. Make the grapevine arch, following the instructions in "Making a Grapevine Arch" on page 49. Make a hanger from the 30-gauge wire and secure it to the back of the center of the arch.

2. Cut two 10-inch pieces of the tapestry ribbon and form each into a 5-inch loop, securing the ends with the transparent tape, following the instructions in "Making Ribbon Loops and Tails" on page 56. Cut the remaining length of ribbon in half, and make two 17-inch tails, gathering and taping the end of each tail and cutting the other end of each at an angle.

3. Hot-glue the ribbon loops and tails in place, as shown in the arrangement, shaping and curving the tails.

4. Hot-glue the sprigs of eucalyptus behind the ribbon loops and tails, following the curve of the grapevine base.

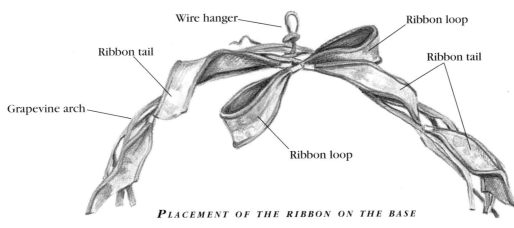

Wire hanger

Ribbon loop

Ribbon tail

Ribbon tail

Grapevine arch

Ribbon loop

PLACEMENT OF THE RIBBON ON THE BASE

5. Referring to "Creating Stems for Heavy Materials" on page 40, make short stems for the pine and spruce cones, pomegranates, artichokes, and tetragonia. Hot-glue each of these in place, using the photograph on pages 138–39 as a guide.

6. Hot-glue one cluster of hydrangea to the left of the center of the arch. Break the other cluster into several pieces, and hot-glue the pieces to the arch where desired.

7. Hot-glue the preserved greenery where needed to hide the mechanics of the arrangement. Hot-glue a few grapevine tendrils to the arrangement as accents.

Save Those Grapevine Tendrils!

I think curly grapevine tendrils provide one of the most interesting accents to dried arrangements. Left to their own devices, these tendrils often end up stuck down between the vines or coming out the back of the wreath arrangement where they can't be seen at all. I hate to have interesting elements go to waste, so if the tendrils don't appear where they will complement the arrangement, I simply snip them off and hot-glue them to another place on the piece where they will be visible. Plus, I save any extra pieces in a box to use as accents in other dried arrangements, wallhangings, or wreaths.

Primary Colors

There are many ways to design topiaries. Some are very structured and compact, while others take on a looser, more casual look. The topiary pictured on page 142 uses a variety of reds, blues, yellows, greens, and other accent colors that would be attractive in many different settings.

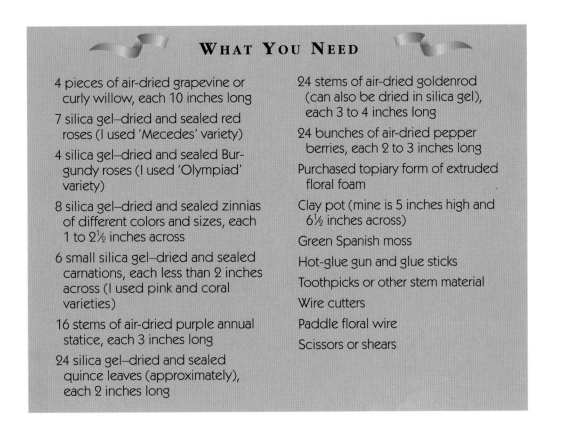

WHAT YOU NEED

4 pieces of air-dried grapevine or curly willow, each 10 inches long

7 silica gel–dried and sealed red roses (I used 'Mecedes' variety)

4 silica gel–dried and sealed Burgundy roses (I used 'Olympiad' variety)

8 silica gel–dried and sealed zinnias of different colors and sizes, each 1 to 2½ inches across

6 small silica gel–dried and sealed carnations, each less than 2 inches across (I used pink and coral varieties)

16 stems of air-dried purple annual statice, each 3 inches long

24 silica gel–dried and sealed quince leaves (approximately), each 2 inches long

24 stems of air-dried goldenrod (can also be dried in silica gel), each 3 to 4 inches long

24 bunches of air-dried pepper berries, each 2 to 3 inches long

Purchased topiary form of extruded floral foam

Clay pot (mine is 5 inches high and 6½ inches across)

Green Spanish moss

Hot-glue gun and glue sticks

Toothpicks or other stem material

Wire cutters

Paddle floral wire

Scissors or shears

WHAT YOU DO

1. Hot-glue the topiary form made from extruded floral foam into the clay pot, as shown. If desired, you can make your own topiary form for this piece, as shown in "Tabletop Topiary Twins" on page 82.

2. Cut the individual pieces of air-dried grapevine slightly longer than the topiary trunk, and bending the grapevine pieces slightly, insert them into the base of the topiary around the trunk and the bottom of the topiary ball. Form

the Spanish moss around the topiary ball with your hands. It isn't necessary to glue the Spanish moss in place because it will be held by the flower stems when they are inserted into the floral form. Cover the base of the topiary with the Spanish moss as well.

3. Make stems for the silica gel–dried flowers, following the instructions in "Adding a Stem" on page 38. I usually begin topiaries by placing flowers of one kind that have visual weight in density and color, and in this case, it is the roses. Hot-glue the flowers as evenly as possible around the Spanish-moss covered floral foam ball so that they extend outward about 1½ inches or so from the surface of the ball. Because this type of floral foam has a hard outer surface, you may have trouble penetrating it with flowers that aren't hot-glued to toothpicks. You can either poke holes in the foam with a toothpick and then insert the flowers with more fragile stems (hot-gluing them in place if you wish), or you can hot-glue a toothpick directly to the stem material and then insert it.

4. Hot-glue the zinnias and carnations around the topiary ball, making sure you create equal gaps between the roses.

5. Fill in the gaps on the topiary ball with the annual statice, leaves, goldenrod, and pepper berries. Cut pieces of the paddle floral wire slightly longer than the pepper berries, and insert these pieces of wire into the foam just beneath or next to the place where the pepper berry stems enter the foam. The wires will give the berries some additional support. Hot-glue the berries to the wires in several places as well.

6. Place small groupings of flowers around the base of the topiary, either hot-gluing the stems of these flowers to the floral foam or inserting them as you did in Steps 3, 4, and 5.

Christmas Centerpiece

I enjoy placing fresh flower arrangements on my dining room table during the Christmas season. Here is one that looks fresh but won't have to be replaced during the holidays.

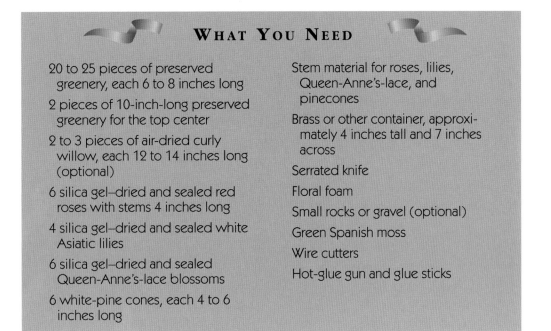

20 to 25 pieces of preserved
greenery, each 6 to 8 inches long

2 pieces of 10-inch-long preserved
greenery for the top center

2 to 3 pieces of air-dried curly
willow, each 12 to 14 inches long
(optional)

6 silica gel–dried and sealed red
roses with stems 4 inches long

4 silica gel–dried and sealed white
Asiatic lilies

6 silica gel–dried and sealed
Queen-Anne's-lace blossoms

6 white-pine cones, each 4 to 6
inches long

Stem material for roses, lilies,
Queen-Anne's-lace, and
pinecones

Brass or other container, approximately 4 inches tall and 7 inches
across

Serrated knife

Floral foam

Small rocks or gravel (optional)

Green Spanish moss

Wire cutters

Hot-glue gun and glue sticks

WHAT YOU DO

1. Using the serrated knife, cut the floral foam to fit the container, and secure it in place following the instructions in "Designing Arrangements" on page 52. Add small rocks to the container to add weight, if desired. Cover the floral foam with the Spanish moss.

2. Insert the longest pieces of greenery and the pieces of curly willow into the center of the floral foam.

3. Add a 4½-inch stem to two of the roses, following the instructions in "Adding a Stem" on page 38. Using to the photograph on the opposite page as a guide for placement, insert the roses into the foam on either side of the arrangement near the center top. Use the height of the roses as a visual guide for determining the length of the other materials in the arrangement. The stem length on the bottom rose just to the right

center of the arrangement is about 2½ inches. Use this as a guide as well.

4. As you hot-glue the lilies to their stems, place them so they angle up slightly, as shown in the diagram.

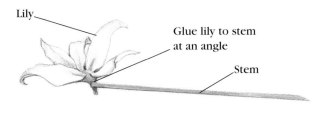

GLUING THE LILY TO THE STEM

5. Working from the top down and moving around the arrangement as you work, place the white Asiatic lilies, Queen-Anne's-lace, and pinecones into the arrangement, using the photograph on the opposite page as a guide.

Side Dressing

People who know what I do for a living sometimes offer me prunings from their yard, and I always happily accept them. I have been surprised to discover that materials I wouldn't think to use can be made into very attractive pieces, and I've learned to appreciate the challenges these materials present. The wild cherry branches I used here were given to me by a local couple. The branches were a bit tricky to use because they were drier than a vine, and I had to handle them gently to avoid snapping them. The payoff was an attractive wreath in a deep walnut color. If you don't have wild cherry, any sturdy vine will work well for this wreath.

WHAT YOU NEED

1 vine wreath, 14 inches in diameter

2 large air-dried pomegranates

3 air-dried bleached okra pods

1 stem of air-dried bleached yarrow

2 sprigs of air-dried burgundy nandina berries, each 6 to 8 inches long

7 medium-sized, oval-shaped, air-dried leaves (I used protea), each 4 to 5 inches long

3 small air-dried poppy pods, each 3 to 4 inches long

6 stems of air-dried off-white filler (I used white top, but peppergrass would also work well), each 4 to 6 inches long

Small, dark, preserved green leaves for contrast (I used poplar), each 3 to 4 inches long

1 yard of wire-edged tapestry ribbon, 2½ inches wide

Scissors or shears

Transparent tape

Wire cutters

Paddle floral wire

Hot-glue gun and glue sticks

WHAT YOU DO

1. Cut a 10-inch piece of the wire-edged tapestry ribbon, and make a 5-inch loop, securing the ends of the ribbon with the transparent tape (see "Making Ribbon Loops and Tails" on page 56).

Cut the remaining length of ribbon in half to make two 13-inch tails. Gather and tape together one end of each ribbon tail, and cut the other end of each at an angle. Establish a working center at the lower right side of the wreath by hot-gluing the ribbons in place, extending the loops and tails out from the working center, as shown in **Diagram 1.**

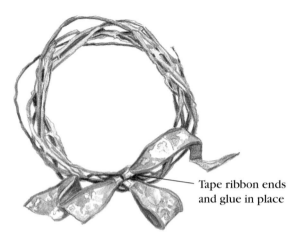

Tape ribbon ends and glue in place

DIAGRAM 1

2. Add a short stem to the pomegranates, following the instructions in "Creating Stems for Heavy Materials" on page 40, and hot-glue them to the working center, as shown in **Diagram 2.** Trim the okra stems to 2 inches, and hot-glue the okra pods in place, as shown.

DIAGRAM 2

3. Cut the stem of the bleached yarrow to 1 inch, and add it next to the pomegranates. Hot-glue the sprigs of nandina berries in place, as shown in **Diagram 2.** If desired, secure the nandina berries to their stems by adding a tiny drop of hot glue to the base of each berry.

4. Add the oval-shaped leaves and poppy pods, referring to the photograph on page 146 for placement. Fill in the arrangement with the off-white filler, and add the dark green leaves where needed for contrast.

SELECTING MATERIALS FOR A WREATH

When choosing materials for a wreath, think about ways to make the grouping interesting. For example, while there is nothing particularly unusual about the individual materials I used in "Side Dressing" on page 146, the variety of shapes, textures, and densities of the materials makes the collection particularly eye-catching. The elongated shapes of the okra pods and the protea leaves are balanced by the dense, solid shapes of the pomegranates and yarrow. The nandina berries and white top are looser in nature and keep the wreath from seeming too heavy. And even though the white top is, by itself, a more delicate material than many of the other materials used in this wreath, it carries appropriate visual weight because of its mass and contrasting color.

To Have and to Hold

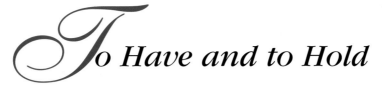

I like to dry the flowers for a wedding bouquet before the wedding. This way, the flowers are at their freshest, and optimum results can be achieved when drying. The bride will have them in that perfect form for any portraits prior to the wedding. If the bridesmaids carry dried bouquets, they can serve as beautiful gifts from the bride!

Bouquet

WHAT YOU NEED

24 to 30 silica gel–dried and sealed roses of various pink shades (I used 'Bride's Dream', 'Pristine', 'Sterling Silver', 'Porcelina', and 'Osiana' varieties)

3 preserved stems of plumosus fern (or other greenery), each 24 inches long

Tussy mussy holder, 8 inches long

Toothpicks

Hot-glue gun and glue sticks

Serrated knife

Floral foam

2⅔ yards of wire-edged pink ribbon, 1½ to 2 inches wide

32-gauge wrapped beading wire

Scissors or shears

Wire cutters

Ruler or yardstick

WHAT YOU DO

1. Hot-glue the toothpicks to the receptacles of the roses. Break the fern into pieces, and hot-glue the toothpicks to the base of the pieces.

2. Using the serrated knife, cut the floral foam to fit inside the tussy mussy holder, extending ¾ inch above the rim.

3. Starting at the top center of the floral foam, insert the roses into the foam so that the top of each rose extends out from the holder about 4 inches. Place the roses close together, as shown in the photo on page 150. Add the fern to fill in gaps and to add touches of wispiness. Continue working down and around the sides of the bouquet, adding the roses and ferns until it is full. Fill in the bottom of the bouquet with the ferns.

4. Cut a piece of ribbon 44 inches long, and make a bow with two 3-inch loops and two 16-inch tails. Make several more loops and tails from the remaining ribbon, following the instructions in "Making Ribbon Loops and Tails" on page 56, and insert them into the first bow, using hot glue to keep them in place. Hot-glue the bow to a toothpick, and insert it into the front of the bouquet.

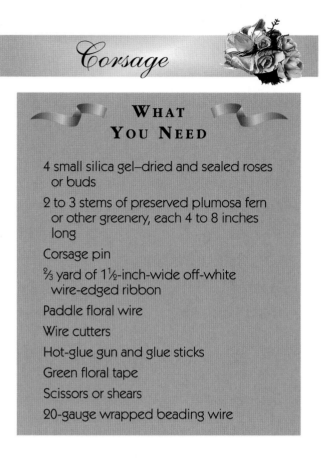

Corsage

WHAT YOU NEED

4 small silica gel–dried and sealed roses or buds

2 to 3 stems of preserved plumosa fern or other greenery, each 4 to 8 inches long

Corsage pin

⅔ yard of 1½-inch-wide off-white wire-edged ribbon

Paddle floral wire

Wire cutters

Hot-glue gun and glue sticks

Green floral tape

Scissors or shears

20-gauge wrapped beading wire

WHAT YOU DO

1. Cut the 20-gauge floral wire into pieces about 6 inches long, and glue one piece of wire to the receptacle of each dried rose. Wrap the wires with the green floral tape. Group the wrapped wires together in your fingers, arranging the roses in a formation similar to the one shown in the photograph on the opposite page. Wrap floral tape around this grouping of stems to hold the stems together.

2. Cut two 8-inch-long pieces of plumosus fern. Remove the lower parts of the fern so that you have bare stems 2 to 3 inches long. Press these stems up against the tackiness of the floral tape in the back of the corsage, and wrap floral tape around this group. Add a few more sprigs of plumosus between the roses and around the bottom of the corsage in the same manner.

3. Make a bow with four 2-inch loops and two 2½-inch tails. Secure the bow, using the beading wire, and tie the tails of the wire around the stems that were taped together in Step 2. Bend the ends of the wire down, wrap them around the other stems, and cover them with the floral tape. Curl the end of the final wire grouping if you wish.

WEARING AND CARRYING DRIED FLOWERS

It's important to remember that dried flowers don't have the flexibility that fresh ones do. Keep this in mind as you pin on a corsage of them, or as you carry them, display them, or store them. At a wedding, for example, make sure that when people hug you, they don't hug your flowers, whether they are worn or carried. Be extra careful not to brush or bump your bouquet against things. And if you have a summer outdoor wedding, for example, watch the humidity levels. If your wedding day happens to be hot and humid, I'd recommend getting the bouquet to a cool, dry place as soon as possible. If the humidity has caused the petals to start to curl, you can place small pieces of cotton balls between the petals to help get them back to their original form as they redry. To help revive the drooping petals, you also can place the bouquet in a covered box with a small uncovered container of silica gel.

 Rose Is a Rose

Roses are wonderful to work with because no two have the same shape or are exactly the same color, and they can be dried in various stages of bloom. With all of that variety, a piece made entirely of roses really comes to life.

WHAT YOU NEED

4 pieces of curly willow, grapevine, or other flexible material, each 24 inches long

16 silica gel–dried and sealed roses in a mixture of deep pink, light pink, lavender, and off-white

30 to 40 air-dried magnolia leaves, each 3 to 4 inches long

5 to 7 tetragonia leaves, each 2 inches long (optional)

Teakettle with boiling water

Hot-glue gun and glue sticks

Toothpicks

Scissors or shears

30-gauge wrapped beading wire

Wire cutters

WHAT YOU DO

1. Using the steam from the teakettle, bend the pieces of curly willow, grapevine, or other flexible material so they have a slight curve or arch to them (see "Bending with Steam" on page 50). Wire together the ends of the arch, and hot-glue the pieces of curly willow together where they touch to add stability to the base of the arrangement.

2. Make stems for the roses by hot-gluing the toothpicks to the receptacles of the roses. Using the photograph above as a guide for placement, glue the stems of the roses to the curly willow base. Glue the magnolia leaves in around the roses, as shown in the photograph. I added the tetragonia leaves for color contrast.

3. Place one of the top horizontal vines on your finger to find the center of balance, as shown in the diagram on the opposite page. Use the beading wire to make a hanger loop, and tie it to the vine at the spot that's the center of balance.

FINDING THE CENTER OF BALANCE

Often the visual center of a wall piece isn't the same as the physical center, or the center of balance. When making a horizontal wall piece, for example, the construction of the base may have more physical weight on one side than on the other. As you add materials to that base, the center of balance may change as well, depending on the materials. Before I make a wire loop for a hanger for a piece, I first find the center of balance by balancing the piece on my finger. I then tie the wire in place at this point so it is snug but not so tight that I can't slide it to the right or left, correcting any balance changes that may occur. When the piece is finished, I again find the center of balance, move the wire loop, add a few more twists so it's tight, and glue it in place.

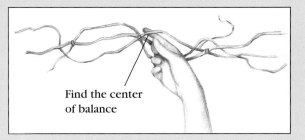

Find the center of balance

Carousel Music

I had this carousel horse for several years before I was willing to take him on. I kept wanting to treat him like a dainty, frilly little thing when he looked more like a Trojan horse. After a friend put a nice antique faux finish on him, a new horse was born and I began to work. This is a project that will also give you an excuse to work with all of the lovely trims and tassels you've been saving for years!

Carousel Horse

WHAT YOU NEED

16 small open roses and 9 rosebuds of various pink shades, silica gel–dried and sealed

Piece of air-dried curly willow, 14 inches long (optional)

1 stem of preserved plumosa fern, 16 inches long

Ceramic or wooden horse

1 piece of fabric (such as fleece, felt, or flannel), 6 × 7 inches

1¼ yards of 1½-inch-wide green wire-edged ribbon

2 yards of ⅜-inch green cording

2 yards of ³⁄₁₆-inch pink cording

14 inches of pink trim with tassels

3 pink rosettes or trim with rosettes

Scissors or shears

Teakettle with boiling water

Ruler or yardstick

Hot-glue gun and glue sticks

WHAT YOU DO

1. Cut a saddle from the 6 × 7-inch piece of fabric, using the pattern in **Diagram 1** and the dimensions of your horse as guides. Using the hot glue, attach the saddle to the back of the ceramic or wooden horse.

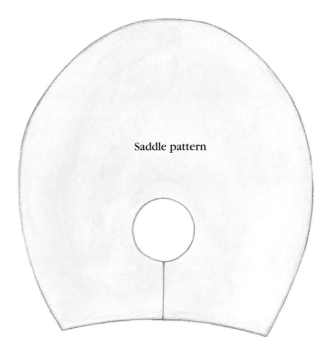

Saddle pattern

DIAGRAM 1

2. Using the steam from the teakettle of boiling water, bend the curly willow to fit the top curve of the horse's rump (see "Bending with Steam" on page 50).

3. Cut two 16-inch pieces of the green wire-edged ribbon, and gather them by holding onto the wire ends and sliding the ribbon edges along the wire until the ribbons measure 8 inches, making ruffles to fit the bottom of the saddle. Fold ½ inch of ribbon over on each end, and add a bead of hot glue along each long edge, so the ribbon doesn't become ungathered. Trim off the ends of wire. Place the remaining piece of ribbon under the horse's belly, and hot-glue it to the bottom edge of the saddle. Hot-glue the gathered pieces of ribbon to the lower edges of the saddle, as shown in the photograph on page 154.

4. Using the measurements in **Diagram 2** as a guide, cut the green and pink cording, and hot glue it in place, as shown, taping the ends before you make cuts. Add the pink trim with the tassels and the pink rosettes, hot-gluing them in place.

BASKET ACCESSORY

Add a little decorated basket to your horse grouping. Find a natural-colored basket and spray-paint it with white paint to give it a white-washed look. Embellish the top by adding silica gel–dried open roses and rosebuds, following the instructions on page 67. Trim with ribbon or cording if you like.

5. Glue a cluster of three roses to the front corners of the saddle on both sides, using the photograph on page 154 as a guide. Place the piece of bent curly willow over the horse's rump (hot-glue it in place if you wish), and hot-glue the remaining open roses to it, as shown in the photograph on page 154. Hot-glue the rosebuds over the top of the horse's head and behind his ears. Break off sprigs of plumosa fern, and glue the sprigs between the roses and buds to fill in any gaps and to cover up any of the mechanics of the piece.

5"

19"

7" nosepiece

20" reins

13"

13"

4" loops

7½"

12"

14"

DIAGRAM 2

Ribbon Accent

WHAT YOU NEED

3 silica gel–dried and sealed roses

3 or 4 small air-dried or preserved leaves

2 yards of 1½-inch-wide pink wire-edged ribbon

1 yard of 1½-inch-wide green wire-edged ribbon

Small wooden box, 2 inches high and 3 inches across

Three 2-inch loops of faux pearls (you can buy them as loops or make your own from pearls sold by the yard)

14-inch strand of fake pearls or other trim

Scissors or shears

Hot-glue gun and glue sticks

WHAT YOU DO

1. Cut a length of the wire-edged pink ribbon 1 yard long, and gather both long edges by holding onto the wire ends and sliding the ribbon edges along the wire until the ribbon measures 14 inches and will cover the sides of the small wooden box. Fold the short ends of the ribbon over, trim off the excess wire, and hot-glue the ribbon to the sides of the box along the top and bottom edges.

2. Snip off 6 to 8 inches of the yard of the wire-edged green ribbon, and set it aside. Gather the remaining green ribbon the same way you gathered the pink ribbon in Step 1, and fold it in half lengthwise to make a ruffle. Hot-glue it to the top side of the box lid. Gather the remaining pink ribbon into a circle to fit the top of the box lid, and glue it in place.

3. Glue the three roses to the center of the box lid, using the photograph on page 154 as a guide. Make little loops 2 to 3 inches long from the green ribbon (see "Mirror Images" on page 64), and fill in the gaps between the roses with the ribbon loops, the dried leaves, and the pearl loops. Hot-glue the 14-inch strand of pearls around the top edge of the box.

Flower Drying Timetable

For detailed information on drying flowers in silica gel, see "Using Silica Gel" on page 20. All flowers are placed face up in silica gel to dry unless the comments direct you to do otherwise. The following drying times are guidelines only. The drying time for any blossom will depend on how turgid the flower is when it is harvested, how large it is, the amount of stem you leave on the blossom, and whether you dry it by itself or with other flowers. The times given are the number of days you should let pass before you check to see if the flower is dry. If the flower is not quite dry after that time, it should be dry enough to hold its form while you re-cover it with silica gel or place its receptacle on a bed of silica gel so that area can continue drying. If you don't find a listing for a specific flower that you'd like to dry, find one that has similar characteristics, and follow those guidelines.

FLOWER	DRYING TIME (DAYS)	COMMENTS
Anemone	5–6	Dry leafy collar separately from blossom and reattach when dry.
Apple Blossom	4–5	Snip flower clusters from branch. Air-dry branch. Remove flower clusters from silica gel when dry; overdrying will cause petals to come loose. Hot-glue flowers to branch when branch is dry. If branch snaps easily, it is dry.
Astilbe	5–6	Dry horizontally to prevent flattening, supporting main stem. Make sure stem is completely dry.
Bachelor's Button	5–6	Cover petals slowly with silica gel to prevent flattening. Make sure petal base inside calyx is dry or petals will droop.
Bleeding Heart	5–6	Leave hearts attached to stalk, and dry horizontally to prevent flattening. Pour silica gel inside hearts before covering to prevent flattening. Shake silica gel out of each heart when dry.
Calla Lily	8–10	Remove center stamen, and dry separately. Reattach stamen when lily is dry. Colors may darken.
Camellia	5–6	Snip flower heads from branches, and dry separately. Dry foliage and branches separately. Color changes may occur.
Carnation	7–8	Cover slowly with silica gel to avoid flattening; get silica gel down inside calyx. Make sure petal base inside calyx is dry or petals will droop. Glue backs of petals to top of calyx to keep them in place.

(continued on page 160)

FLOWER	DRYING TIME (DAYS)	COMMENTS
Chrysanthemum	5–7	Petals often come loose when removing flowers from silica gel; reattach to flower using hot glue.
Clematis	5–6	Clean carefully after drying, removing all silica gel particles and dust from front and back petals. Colors may darken. Keep dry.
Columbine	3–5	Petals may come loose when removing flower from silica gel; reattach to flower using hot glue. Clean thoroughly. Keep dry.
Coneflower	5–6	Dry face-down to retain contour of petals. Remove grains of silica gel from center with a toothpick. Colors may darken.
Coralbells	4–5	Remove stubborn grains of silica gel from inside individual bells with a toothpick. Clean with sand.
Cornflower	5–6	See Bachelor's Button on page 159.
Daffodil	5–7	Remove carefully from silica gel or petals may tear or come loose. Make sure receptacle is dry. Clean thoroughly. Keep dry. Support petals during storage.
Dahlia	5–10	Drying times vary for different types of dahlias. If left too long in silica gel, petals will come off. Test flower stalk at base of flower for dryness. Clean carefully. Remove stubborn grains of silica gel from center with a toothpick or small watercolor brush. Petals tear easily.
Daisy	4–7	Petals shrink while drying. If left too long in silica gel, petals may come off. When center is dry, uncover flower, and place on a bed of fresh silica gel in a covered container for a few days. (See also Shasta Daisy on page 163.)
Delphinium	5–7	Dry horizontally, supporting stalk as it is covered, and pouring silica gel between petals. Save petals that come loose as you pour off silica gel; reglue (using hot glue) loose petals to flower. Clean petals carefully and thoroughly.
Dogwood	3–4	One of the fastest and easiest flowers to dry. Small to medium blossoms work best; large ones tend to get floppy. Snip flowers from branch. Air-dry branch. Reattach flowers to branch when both are dry.
Flowering Quince	5–7	Take cuttings in early spring, and bury branch with blossoms intact in silica gel. Also take cuttings in summer when leaves are larger. Leaf colors may lighten.

FLOWER	DRYING TIME (DAYS)	COMMENTS
Foliage	3–10	Leaves can be left on stem, such as a rose, to dry. (Flower is dried separately.) Check most dense part of stem to test for dryness; if not completely dry, leaves will droop.
Forget-Me-Not	3–4	Don't overdry or flowers and petals will come loose from stalk. Make sure fuzzy leaves and stems are cleaned well. Blues and pinks dry bright and clear.
Forsythia	5–7	Blossoms dry quickly; woody branch needs more time to dry completely. Carefully remove from silica gel when flowers are dry or blossoms will come off branch. Clean carefully using a soft watercolor brush and gently blowing on petals. Reattach loose flowers to branch if needed. Yellow flowers tend to fade quickly.
Foxglove	6–8	Dry horizontally to prevent flattening. Fill each bell with silica gel, or snip off bells with fingernails, dry them upright, and reglue bells to stalk when both have dried.
Fruit Blossom	4–5	See Apple Blossom on page 159.
Gerbera Daisy	7–8	Remove from silica gel when center is dry. If left too long in silica gel, petals will come off. Glue loose petals back to flower. Run circle of hot glue around back of flower, connecting backs of petals to the sepals.
Gloriosa Lily	5–7	Good color when dried. Leave a 1/2-inch stem on back of flower. May be hard to find, but worth the trouble.
Goldenrod	5–7	Harvest when still a bit green to keep flower tassels intact when dry. Dry horizontally, supporting stalk to prevent flattening.
Hellebore	5–6	Dries nicely. Unique shape. Flower stays nice and crisp when dried and has nice color variations.
Hydrangea	8–12	Break apart mophead into smaller clusters to dry. Stalks are dense and will take longer to dry, so dry them separately.
Iris	5–8	Fragile when dry. Handle carefully, clean well, and keep in dry environment. Smaller irises are easier to work with.
Johnny-Jump-Ups	3–4	See Pansy on page 162.
Larkspur	4–6	Dry horizontally, supporting to prevent flattening. Clean blossoms thoroughly. If petals come loose, hot-glue them back to the blossom.

(continued on page 162)

FLOWER	DRYING TIME (DAYS)	COMMENTS
Lilac	5–7	Cut large clusters from main stems to dry. Air-dry stems. Hot-glue blossoms to stems. Clean thoroughly.
Lily	5–8	Trim stem to ½ inch to expedite drying. Remove all dew from inside petals to prevent discoloration. Dry pistils, stamens, and anthers separately in silica gel.
Lily of the Valley	5–7	Dry horizontally to prevent flattening. Fill each bell on stalk with silica gel. Color usually turns creamy.
Marigold	5–7	Gently press calyx into shallow bed of silica gel and cover, supporting petals. Fill center of calyx with silica gel. Petals will shrink, and color may fade over time.
Mock Orange	5–7	Dry clusters of flowers and leaves together in long or short sprays. Choose clusters of blossoms that are not too mature to prevent petals from coming loose. White blossom will dry white.
Monarda	5–6	Dry two flower heads. Then remove petals from one flower head to hot-glue to the other to make blossom look full. Petals may shrink and fall from center of flower; if so, reattach them with hot glue.
Pansy	3–4	Handle gently. Get silica gel up under back side of petals and around sepals. Keep dry.
Peony	5–8	Carefully sift silica gel down between center petals of semidouble and double blooms so they hold their form. Clean flowers well when dry.
Poinsettia	7–9	Dry flower heads or bracts with short stems. Before drying, singe stem end with flame to stop milky sap from flowing. Carefully remove dried flowers from silica gel or red leaves will tear. Clean each leaf carefully and well.
Primrose	3–4	Spoon silica gel inside little cup created by sepals before placing in silica gel. Clean well and keep dry. Reds, blues, and purples darken; pastels retain bright colors.
Queen-Anne's-Lace	3–4	Harvest before flower head becomes too mature for full blossom. Place in drying container face-down on shallow bed of silica gel and gently sift gel over flower head to retain umbel shape.

FLOWER	DRYING TIME (DAYS)	COMMENTS
Ranunculus	5–7	Clean carefully and keep dry. Petals will be papery thin when dry, but colors are nice.
Redbud	4–5	Blossoms are too small and fragile to clean individually; tap branch with pencil to knock silica gel residue loose, and blow on blossoms to dust them off.
Rose	6–10	Make sure all dew is removed from between petals before drying. Try to loosen tight centers (except if you are drying buds). Colors will darken in most varieties.
Rudbeckia	5–7	Clean sepals well. Reattach any petals that come loose. Colors remain bright.
Shasta Daisy	6–7	Midsummer variety dries crisper than smaller earlier varieties, and petals stay intact better.
Snapdragon	5–7	Pinch individual florets off stalk (except for tight buds), fill throats of florets with silica gel, and dry separately from stalk, getting silica gel up under throats so florets hold their form. Clean florets carefully and hot-glue to dried stalk. Keep dry.
Snow-on-the-Mountain	8–10	Before drying, singe stem end with flame to stop milky sap from flowing. Handle clusters carefully when dry. Expect green color to fade over time.
Spirea	5–7	Select branches with immature blossoms. Cut length of branch with flower clusters and leaves. Dry horizontally to prevent flattening. Clean by tapping stem with pencil and gently blowing on flowers. Remove stubborn particles of silica gel with a toothpick.
Sunflower	7–14	Larger flowers will take longer to dry. Yellow color of petals will turn white over time. In some varieties, petals become almost transparent.
Sweet Pea	4–6	Blossoms dry papery thin, so clean and handle carefully. Dry leaves and vines to add to blossoms. Keep dry.
Tulips	5–8	Start with fresh flowers a few shades darker than desired; colors may soften. If anthers come loose, glue to filament.
Zinnia	4–6	Pick when in full bloom. Work silica gel between petals with end of watercolor brush. Color changes may occur.

Acknowledgments

This book evolved to be what it is because of the help of many people. First and foremost, a big thanks to my mom and dad for putting up with my collections all those many years ago, encouraging my creativity and exposing their children to other aspects of life that existed beyond the walls of our little community. Thanks to the rest of my family for their unending encouragement and support, too. Thanks to Geneal Condon, wherever you may be, for a wonderful article in National Geographic that made for some good fun for a child and inspired an adult to make drying flowers her passion.

Thanks to Mark Koch for putting me in touch with some interesting reading material, and thanks to all of the folks who were willing to take time to help me get the technical details accurate: Rob Edmunds; Wallace Gwinn, Ph.D., Utah Geological and Mineral Survey, Provo, Utah; Dr. Philip Lee, Department of Biology, Roanoke College; Dr. Don Rimstidt, Professor of Geochemistry, Virginia Institute of Technology; and Dr. Alan McDaniel, Associate Professor, Department of Horticulture, Virginia Institute of Technology. Thanks to Sheila Lowe at Eagle Chemical for her priceless explanation of how silica gel is made.

Thanks to the folks at Rodale Press for believing this book was a good idea, too, with a special thanks to Managing Editor Cheryl Tetreau for her guidance with my writing and for giving me a lot of freedom to do what I needed to do to put this book together; to Marya Amig and Mary Green for their fine editing skills; to Jennifer Hornsby and Erana Bumbardatore for their excellent copyediting; to Margaret Lydic for her editorial insights; to photographer Mitch Mandel and his assistant, Glenn Milano, for two fun weeks when we shot the photos for the book; and to Trish Field for her wonderful photo styling skills. Thanks to Susan Egbert for her wonderful illustrations and to art director Trish Field, book designer Marta Strait, and layout designer Dale Mack for their abilities to pull everything together to design a beautiful book.

Thanks to the other individuals who supplied me with wonderful varieties of flowers that I planted, grew, and used for some of the designs in this book: Elizabeth Dean at Wilkerson Mill Gardens, Mary Anne Rennebohm at Heard Gardens, André Viette at Viette Farm and Nursery, Deborah DeMichaels at Van Dyke's Flower Farms, Kathy Edmunds at Edmunds' Roses, and Klehm Nursery for peonies. Thanks to Sonny Campbell for helping to get everything in the ground.

Thanks to Cindi Lou MacMackin at the Inn at Burwell Place, and to Judy Damon and Herb Detweiler for being great hosts and for allowing us to invade their premises, and a special thanks to Judy for her help with photo styling and for paintings that helped tell the story. Thanks to Carol Phillips for turning a Trojan horse into one fit for a carousel and to the folks at Dunman Floral for filling in my flower gaps. And thanks to Mike Jefferson for his invaluable computer assistance and for helping me through the "years of the book" in every other way imaginable.

Sources

André Viette Farm and Nursery
Long Meadow Rd.
P.O. Box 1109
Fishersville, VA 22939
(540) 943-2315
Perennials, including peonies, irises, flowering shrubs, ground covers, daylilies, and hostas. Catalog and garden handbook includes color photographs and tips for garden design. A $5 charge for catalog puts you on the mailing list for 3 years.

Dutch Gardens
P.O. Box 200
Adelphia, NJ 07710-0200
(800) 818-3861
Bulbs, tubers, and perennials. Free color catalog.

Edmunds' Roses
6235 S.W. Kahle Rd.
Wilsonville, OR 97070
(888) 481-7673
Hybrid tea, grandiflora, floribunda, and climbing roses. Free color catalog.

Heard Gardens Ltd.
5355 Merle Hay Rd.
Johnston, IA 50131
(515) 276-4533
Lilacs: An extensive variety of colors and sizes of bare, own-root (not grafted) cultivars. Catalog with descriptions of varieties available for $2.

Heronswood Nursery Ltd.
7530 N.E. 288th St.
Kingston, WA 98346-9502
(360) 297-4172
Perennials, shrubs, trees, and vines. Extensive number of varieties offered. Two-year subscription to catalog for $5.

Klehm Nursery
4210 N. Duncan Rd.
Champaign, IL 61822
(800) 553-3715
Tree peonies, peonies, perennials, ornamental grasses, woody plants, daylilies, and hostas. Catalog with some color photographs and illustrations available for $4 (refundable with order).

Park's Seed Co.
1 Parkton Ave.
Greenwood, SC 29647
(800) 845-3369
Seeds for annuals and perennials. Free color catalog.

Spring Hill Nurseries
110 W. Elm St.
Tipp City, OH 45371
(800) 582-8527
Bulbs, perennials, woody ornamentals, and roses. Free color catalog.

Thompson & Morgan
P.O. Box 1308
Jackson, NJ 08527
(800) 274-7333
Seeds for annuals and perennials. Free color catalog.

Van Dyck's Flower Farms
P.O. Box 430
Brightwaters, NY 11718
(800) 248-2852
Daffodils, tulips, lilies, and other flowering bulbs. Free color catalog.

White Flower Farm
P.O. Box 50
Litchfield, CT 06759-0050
(800) 503-9624
Perennials. Free color catalog.

Wilkerson Mill Gardens
Department R
9595 Wilkerson Mill Rd.
Palmetto, GA 30268
(770) 463-2400
Hydrangeas, trees, and shrubs. Descriptive catalog with cultivating tips available for $3.

Index

Note: Page numbers in **boldface** indicate photographs; those in *italic* indicate illustrations.